So You Think You Know About Cats?

So You Think You Know About Cats?

An All-in-One Guide for Felines and Their Humans

Ronald Rosen, DVM and Francine Hornberger

CITADEL PRESS
Kensington Publishing Corp.
www.kensingtonbooks.com

CITADEL PRESS BOOKS are published by

Kensington Publishing Corp.
850 Third Avenue
New York, NY 10022

All Kensington titles, imprints, and distributed lines are available at special quantity
discounts for bulk purchases for sales promotions, premiums, fund-raising, educational,
or institutional use. Special book excerpts or customized printings can also be created
to fit specific needs. For details, write or phone the office of the Kensington special
sales manager: Kensington Publishing Corp., 850 Third Avenue, New York, NY 10022,
attn: Special Sales Department; phone 1-800-221-2647.

First Printing: May 2006

10 9 8 7 6 5 4 3 2 1

Printed in the United States of America

Library of Congress Control Number: 2005938599

ISBN 0-8065-2749-8

*For my dear departed cat Brownie, who was the gentlest,
sweetest soul I have ever been privileged to meet.* —RR

*For my sister, Tanya Hornberger, who loves cats
more than anyone I know.* —FH

Contents

Contents

Acknowledgments

Dr. Ronald Rosen

I would like to thank my collaborator, Francine Hornberger, for the opportunity to participate in this wonderful project. Special thanks to my children, Alex and Michelle, for all the love and joy they bring me. Thanks also to all my clients at the North Shore Animal Hospital and the South Bellmore Veterinary Group for all the faith and trust they have shown me in caring for their pets over the years. My biggest thanks goes to my wife, Mia, for all her love, support, and advice over the years. Her caring, gentle ways and her uncompromising love of cats and all animals has taught me to be a better husband, father, and veterinarian.

My last thanks go to my fab-five felines—Brittany, Cody, Sabrina, Lily, and Will—who make me laugh every day and who generously allow me to share their home with them.

Francine Hornberger

I would like to thank Gary Goldstein for signing this project and to Arthur Maisel at Citadel for all his hard work in making it an actual book. Thanks also to my friends and family for your patience and support while I worked to get it done. Thanks also goes to my collaborator and vet to my cats, Dr. Ronald Rosen, for his invaluable input and instruction as well as to the staff at North Shore Animal Hospital in Bayside, New York, for keeping my two girls healthy and happy!

A special thank-you goes out to all those who contributed photographs of and funny stories about their cats, including Colette Carey, Lucille Collins, Nicole Dauenhauer, Cheryl Hackert, the Hornberger family, the Mayer family, Karen and Ian Chow-Miller, the Pearlstein family, Jennifer and Don Riddell, Stephanie and Rupert Ruding-

Bryan, Michele Santelices, Maria Tahim, and Pete and Mindy Walker. And I would be utterly remiss not to thank Fluffy, Josie, Casey, Weedy, Katya, and all the fabulous felines I have known and loved, and from whom I have learned so much. Their antics have entertained, delighted, and indeed, educated me.

Last but not least, thank you to my family and friends for their patience and support as I completed my work on this book — especially to my husband, Christopher, whose love and encouragement make all my creations possible, and to my brand new daughter, Madeleine, who inspires me every day.

Introduction

The ideal of calm exists in a sitting cat.
—Jules Reynard

So you think you know your cat, do you? Okay, if that's the case, then of course you can easily answer these questions:

- How many different "meows" does your kitty have?
- Just who does your cat think she is when she hisses?
- How often does she need to see the vet?
- How often should you scoop her litter box?
- Can you toilet-train your cat?
- When's the best time to spay or neuter your kitten?

Could you answer all of them? Chances are, some were easy, some were not, but all made you wonder. And that's just what having a cat in your life is like!

If you're one of the lucky people whom more than 70 million cats in the United States alone permits to live in his house or apartment with him, you probably have a ton of questions just like these—some you can answer and some you can't. Naturally, you'd like to think you know a little something about your cat. But as friends to our fabulous felines, we know all too well how incredibly elusive they can be. Of course that doesn't mean we don't know anything about them at all.

But exactly how much do we really know? And how much do they ever really let on for us to be able to guess?

One thing is for sure: To be the best possible companions to our cats, we should know as much as we can about them. And that's where this book comes in. The more you know, the more you will understand your feline friend, and the more he or she will show his or her appreciation through heartfelt head butts, numerous loving nibbles, and perfectly contented purrs.

> *A cat can be trusted to purr when she is pleased, which is*
> *more than can be said for human beings.*
> —William Randolph Inge

CALLING ALL CAT LOVERS!

It's time to put your knowledge to the test with this fun and entertaining quiz-and-reference book—and also learn a lot about your fabulous feline—or felines.

Now this is not your ordinary cat manual. Yes, it is a guidebook, in a way, but it's also entirely interactive. It doesn't just impart knowledge and information; rather, it challenges you to really *think* about what you're taking in—in a very fun way—by quizzing you.

It's also different from other quiz books. You won't get the typical one-word or one-thought answers with this book. Instead, you'll find extensive answers jam-packed with invaluable information. In other words, you won't simply learn that your cat has a vocabulary of at least *twenty—if not more—sounds* or that she thinks *she's a snake* when she hisses or that she should see the vet *at least once a year* when she's grown—and several times a year when she's a kitten—or that his litter box needs to be *scooped daily* or that she *can be toilet-trained*, if she decides she wants to be, or that a kitten should be *spayed or neutered by six months* and sometimes earlier—you'll find out exactly *why*. Inside, find forty quizzes on various topics and in several formats including multiple-choice, true or false, and match-ups. Each quiz section opens with an informative section opener, but you won't find many—if any—of the answers to the quiz there! You'll be asked to add up your score, then report to the scoring section at the back of the book to get an overall score for all the quizzes you have taken and a summary of exactly how much you really know about your cat. On top of that, you'll find helpful sidebars to teach you everything from how to find a vet to the mysteries of catnip.

There are lots of ways to enjoy this book. You can read it straight through and get a vast overview on cat ownership. You can jump to the sections you need when you have a specific question. You can sit and observe your cat as you try to answer the questions on your own—or you can bond with fellow feline aficionados by doing the quizzes in groups—a lot more fun than Pictionary or Charades at a dinner party for cat lovers!

Whatever way you choose to enjoy this book, we hope you'll have fun taking the quizzes and also learning more about this amazing and beloved species that we cat lovers could never live without!

> *By associating with the cat, one only risks*
> *becoming richer.*
> —Colette

So You Think
You Know About Cats?

1

Are You Really a Cat Person?

Never send a man to do a cat's job.
—Garfield, from his 1987 Christmas special

Many of us who live with felines like to think we're cat lovers. And if you went through the trouble of buying this book, there's a pretty good chance that you're a bigger fan of cats than someone who may not have made the effort. But how much of a cat person are you really?

To get to the bottom of that, and to see how much being a cat companion means to you, you have to ask yourself exactly what you would do for your cat? Would you forgo making purchases for yourself so you could afford top-of-the-line kibble for your kitty? Would you dump a significant other if he or she confesses to actually being more of a dog person? And who exactly is listed as the main beneficiary in your will?

In all seriousness, those of us who are true cat lovers have come to make some concessions in our lives in order to make the lives of our cats as enjoyable, comfortable, and in some cases, indulgent as possible. And we aren't sorry about it either. It doesn't mean we're freaks or fanatics, though those people do exist—and trust us, as vain as cats are, it makes them quite uncomfortable to be objects of their humans' obsessions. There's a line between love and loving too much, a true cat person clearly sees and respects it.

Want to know where you fall on the grand scale of cat lovers? Take the following quiz to find out!

CAT FACT
Petting a cat can actually reduce your blood pressure.

QUIZ #1

Answer the following multiple-choice questions to see if you really love cats as much as you say you do!

1. You notice a golf ball sitting in the middle of your living room floor. Do you . . . ?

   a. Get annoyed and throw it away.
   b. Leave it there so you can yell at your spouse for being a slob when he or she gets home.
   c. Leave it there. You suspect your cat has made a toy of it and will come back to it when she is ready.
   d. Pick it up and place it out of "harm's way." You don't want someone to trip over it!

2. A person you've just started to date who you think might have potential tells you he or she dislikes cats. Do you . . . ?

   a. Disregard the comment. In the long run, does it really matter if your partner likes cats or not when you share so many other common interests?
   b. Proceed with the relationship—but with high caution. A person who dislikes cats may have other serious issues.
   c. End the relationship then and there. There can be nothing redeeming about a person who doesn't like cats.
   d. Find out what the person dislikes about cats and try to fix any misperceptions he or she may have.

3. Which is *not* an appropriate place to kiss your cat?

   a. On his paws
   b. On the top of his head
   c. Right smack on the mouth
   d. None of the above

4. You're expecting company in fifteen minutes, and you have yet to make the bed. Trouble is, your oversized tabby has taken full advantage of the bumpy, bunched-up blankies to enjoy a nap. Do you . . . ?

   a. Toss him off the bed so you can finish straightening up.
   b. Poke at him hoping to rouse him so he'll jump off the bed on his own. If not, try again in a few minutes.
   c. Spray him with a water bottle to startle him awake.
   d. Close the room off to company by closing the door, and let him sleep.

5. How many photos do you take of your cat on average?

   a. None.
   b. Maybe a couple a month.
   c. Maybe a couple a day.
   d. I had to buy a digital camera because I was spending all my money on film developing.

6. Your cat has a habit of pulling all the Q-tips out of the bathroom dispenser and tossing them all over the floor. You think this is:

   a. Absolutely the cutest thing.
   b. Grounds for putting her up for adoption.
   c. Annoying, but the laugh it gives you is worth the inconvenience.
   d. An irritating menace.

7. Do you allow your cat to sleep with you?

    a. I love falling asleep with my cat purring next to me.
    b. I don't mind my cat sleeping with me, provided she doesn't take up more than her fair share of bed space.
    c. I'd much rather share my bed with my cat than my spouse.
    d. A cat in my bed? That would be like sleeping with the Tasmanian Devil.

8. How often do you completely change your cat's litter box—and we're not talking scooping here, but scrubbing and disinfecting the box and replacing all the litter:

    a. Every day.
    b. Once a week.
    c. Once a month.
    d. You mean scooping isn't enough?

9. Do you ever wish you could bring your cat out with you—like to work or to run errands or anything like that?

    a. I'd love to smuggle my cat into work and keep her under my desk.
    b. I *do* take my cat to work with me and often—please don't tell my boss!
    c. Honestly, as much as I like my cat, I don't mind taking a break from her sometimes.
    d. Honestly, as much as my cat likes me, she doesn't mind having a break from me sometimes.

10. When you're on vacation, how often do you call your answering machine to comfort your cat with the sound of your voice?

    a. Maybe once or twice, after I check my messages.
    b. At least once a day—if not more.
    c. I never call home when I'm away.
    d. I don't take vacations from my cat.

Answers to Quiz #1

1. C. The cat toy industry is certainly a healthy one, but as any cat lover knows, a cat's favorite toys are often found just around the house. A golf ball, for instance, can bring an energetic kitty hours of joy as she bats it about in her own rendition of kitty soccer. Of course, your cat doesn't want to have to *look* for these toys when she wants to play with them. Where's the fun in that? A cat is an impulsive creature, and the most pleasure for her comes when she spots an object and gets inspired to play with it. So if you're the type who doesn't mind an odd object here and there out of place in your home, you get your cat.

2. D. It's definitely a red flag when someone you're dating confesses to not liking cats. There's no possibility of a cat-less future for you, so it almost seems like it's best to not make any kind of time investment with a person like this. However, many people who don't like cats may just not understand them. So instead of throwing away something that could work, you owe it to yourself, your cat—and cats everywhere—to try to change his or her misperceptions. If the person doesn't come around after you've at least made an effort to win him or her, then by all means, dump away—and find a person who shares your passion!

3. D. As any cat lover knows, it's fine and acceptable to kiss your cat just about anywhere on his adorable body. If he minds where you're planting one, he'll let you know. For example, some cats are very sensitive about their paws and may object to being kissed on them, though they will generally permit it as they know how irresistible those feet are to their humans!

4. D. There's no rule saying that you have to tour every human who comes to your home through each and every room. The bedroom is a private place anyway. If your cat is having a nap, let him sleep—especially if he's all curled up and cute. Just be sure you don't close the door all the way. Keep it ajar so that he can come and greet visitors when he's properly rested and ready!

5. B, C, and even D are all acceptable answers here. Your cat does so many precious things all the time, you probably could make a full-time job of being a pussy paparazzi. And hey, that digital camera comes in handy for lots of other things, right? If you take no pictures of your cat at all, though, are you really appreciating all the effort she expends to be so ridiculously cute? Think about it!

6. C. Part of the territory of sharing your home with a cat is that she could do anything at any time. She's insatiably curious about everything. Imagine living with a toddler who can run as fast, jump as high, and with such sublime "paw" dexterity. When you live with a cat, there's a certain amount of cat-proofing you have to do (see page 41), and there are going to be things you'll never be able to anticipate until they actually happen. Getting angry isn't going to help anything. And think of it this way: Is it such a bad habit to securely close the lid once you're finished using the Q-tips?

7. A. The key to accepting your cat in your bed is to essentially accept it on her terms. Anyone who's shared a bed with a cat knows that "sharing" is the human's role; the cat will sprawl out in whatever position makes her the most comfortable. If you sleep with your cat, appreciate what she gives you. A cat who purrs loudly enough might even drown out the less-appealing sound of a snoring spouse. But getting back to that "loving too much bit," your cat does not want to get in the way of your marriage or relationship. If you prefer sleeping with your cat over your partner, you may want to seek some counseling.

8. B. As particular as your cat may be, he does not want you spending every last dime you have on cat litter when you can be buying him food or treats or toys. If a cat's box gets scooped daily, he'll be perfectly happy with you actually changing all the litter once a week—or even every ten days. Letting it go much more than that will be unpleasant for him as even with clumping litter, traces of urine are still left behind. But don't worry: If you let it go too long, he will gladly and, he feels, graciously let you know you have by urinating or defecating just out-side his box.

9. While C and D are both acceptable, D is the better answer. (Give yourself an extra bonus point in your score for this quiz if you answered D.) Remember, there is a line between loving your cat—and loving your cat too much. Your cat does not want to sit in a carrier all day just to be close to you. She wants to be able to explore and play and nap and eat on her own turf, whether you're there with her or not. It isn't that she doesn't love you, but when you give her a chance to miss you, she realizes how much she really does love you.

10. A. Believe it or not, your cat does get lonely for you sometimes. As long as you're checking in anyway once or twice while you're away, why not treat her to the sound of your voice. She'll appreciate it. Of course, if you do it too much, she will feel smothered—so try and rein yourself in, would you!

Give yourself a point for every correct answer. SCORE:_____

Now turn to page 217 to record your score, then head to the next quiz.

2

Cat Characteristics I

I believe cats to be spirits come to earth. A cat, I am sure,
could walk on a cloud without coming through.
—Jules Verne

As any cat lover can guess, there's more to cats then meets the eye. The feline species is one of the most intricately, ingeniously designed group of mammals there is. No part of your cat exists by accident; she has no superfluous traits.

Take for example your cat's whiskers. Sure they make her look like she's wearing an adorably silly mustache, but there's a lot more to that facial fringe than pure aesthetics. Your cat's whiskers are among her most important pieces of physical equipment. But what exactly do they *do*? Your cat uses her whiskers to detect air movements, to protect her eyes, and also to help her orient to her surroundings. Take a look at her whiskers: They are as long as your cat's body is wide. She knows that if her whiskers don't clear a tempting opening, she's not going to clear it either. As a real testament to the power of a cat's whiskers, it has been suggested that if one of a mother cat's kittens gets a little too nosy about his surroundings, she might actually bite off those whiskers to keep him close to her. Not to worry: Whether trimmed by Mama or by a school-age barber-wannabe with a pair of scissors and no doll hair to experiment on, a cat's whiskers will grow back if they are cut.

Of course, it's not just her whiskers that serve double-duty of maximum cuteness and amazing function. So you think you know about the physical makeup of your cat? This quiz, and those that follow, will clue you in to what you know and teach you things that may surprise you!

CAT FACT

All cats have an extra eyelid in each eye. In a healthy cat, the third eyelid will not be visible. So, if you can see your cat's third eyelid, call the vet right away as he may have injured himself or have a fever or illness.

QUIZ #2

Think you know all about your cat's unique features? Take this quiz to see!

1. Where is a cat's sense of touch strongest?

   a. In her paws
   b. In her whiskers
   c. Both A and B
   d. Neither A nor B

2. What's so special about a cat's nose?

   a. It's interminably kissable.
   b. It changes color with your cat's mood.
   c. It can help humans determine if their cats are in peak health or feeling under the weather.
   d. The pattern on the nose pad is unique to every cat.

3. Which of the following mammals is a cat's brain most similar to:

   a. A mouse
   b. A horse
   c. A dog
   d. A human

4. How many olfactory ("smelling") cells does a cat have?

   a. Between 60 and 80 million
   b. Between 15 and 25 million
   c. Between 5 and 10 million
   d. About 1 million

5. Can cats see color?

   a. No, they are color blind and only see in black and white.
   b. They can only see blue and green.
   c. They can see blue, green, and red, but nothing else.
   d. They can see the world in all its vibrant color.

6. A cat sees:

   a. Poorly—she mostly relies on her sense of smell.
   b. Just what's in front of her.
   c. 180 degrees around her.
   d. 360 degrees around her.

7. How many muscles does a cat have in each of her ears?

   a. 6
   b. 20
   c. 25
   d. 30

8. How many whiskers do cats typically have?

   a. 12
   b. 24
   c. 48
   d. 64

9. How about teeth? How many do you think?

   a. 20
   b. 30

    c. 40

    d. 50

10. How many bones does your cat have in her whole body?

    a. 150

    b. 175

    c. 206

    d. 230

Answers to Quiz #2

1. C. Cats have touch receptors all over their bodies, but their sense of touch is most concentrated in their paw pads and whiskers. That they feel things with their pads is pretty obvious, but most people don't realize that not only can cats feel things with their whiskers, but that their adorable face-framers can feel movements two thousand times smaller than the width of a human hair!

2. If you said A, C, or D, give yourself 1 point. If you said B, we have to ask you: Do you really think a cat would ever so obviously give away its mood? Shame on you! There's no doubt that your cat's nose is one of the most kissable aspects of her face. And most cat owners know that a cold, wet nose means a healthy cat. But there's more going on with that delectably charming nose pad than most humans are aware. Incredibly, the ridges your cat has on her nose pad form a pattern (called a nasolabiogram) as unique as a human fingerprint. Not that she'd ever permit you to dip her nose in ink for identification or anything that preposterous. Don't believe us? See for yourself. If you have more than one cat living with you, grab a magnifying glass and hold it up to the nose of each. You'll see!

3. D. You didn't really believe that Jerry was smarter than Tom, did you? Don't believe everything you see in the cartoons—or on TV for that matter. Sure, Mr. Ed could talk, but as far as horses go with being great intellects . . . well, you couldn't imagine a cat ever agreeing to have its back mounted or to hauling a carriage or cargo. And of course you knew cats were much smarter than dogs. But the fact that a cat's brain is most like a human's is what makes the most sense. Of course, it's only part of the reason you feel so connected to your cat.

4. A. Cats are famous for their incredible sense of smell. The average cat has between 60 and 80 million olfactory cells, while the average human only has 5 to 20 million. And that's plenty. Do you think she would ever go near you or anyone for that matter if your cat had more than 80 million olfactory cells? It's not likely.

5. If you answered either B or C, give yourself 1 point. It used to be that specialists believed that cats could only see in black and white, but no more. Through behavioral studies, scientists have been able to discern that cats have some color-seeing ability. There is also still some debate over whether cats can also see red, and that inability to see red is what makes the biggest difference.

6. C. Like her sense of smell, a cat's eyesight is extremely well developed. True, cats are farsighted—meaning your cat can see something across the room or yards away outside, but she can't see directly under her nose. Her vision is also excellent at night.

7. D. A cat's thirty ear muscles allow her outer ear to move through an arc of about 180 degrees, which makes it easy for her to pinpoint the exact location of a sound. Also, cats can hear sounds about two octaves higher than what the human ear is able to detect.

8. C. A cat has twenty-four of those amazing whiskers. They are arranged on each side of her face, twelve on each side. These twelve are arranged in two rows, and the upper rows can actually move independently of the bottom rows, which helps explain how they can be used so effectively as "radars."

9. B. Never doubt that your feline friend is a true-blue carnivore. Like her big cat relatives, your cat's mouth is designed to rend meat to shreds. Your cat has thirty teeth in all: twelve incisors, ten premolars, four canines, and four molars.

10. D. With all the improbable places they can slink in and out of, sometimes it's hard to believe your cat has any bones at all. But it's because she has so many bones for her size, 230 in all, that she's able to be such a contortionist: Having more small bones allows her to enjoy much more flexibility than if she had larger bones. It's interesting to note that in older cats, sometimes bones fuse together, making for less bones, which is why you'll see varying numbers when it comes to cats' bone count.

Give yourself a point for every correct answer. SCORE:_____

Now turn to page 217 to record your score, then head to the next quiz.

3

Cat Breeds

*To understand a cat, you must realize that he has his own
gifts, his own viewpoint, even his own morality.*
—Lilian Jackson Braun

No two cats are exactly alike—and neither are any two cat breeds.
About forty domesticated cat breeds are recognized by the Cat
Fancier's Association, the "World's Largest Registry of Pedigreed
Cats." Of these, thirty-seven are classified as show breeds, while the
remaining ones are cataloged as "miscellaneous," pending show breed
status.

Of course, unless you are looking to get involved in the cat show
circuit, whether a breed is "show" or "miscellaneous" class probably
has little bearing on why you wish to acquire a pure-bred cat. Chances
are, you've fallen in love with a particular variety—for its coat, its tem-
perament—and know that it will make for a perfect companion for you
and your family.

There are a few things you need to consider when obtaining a pure-
bred cat, some of which will be covered further in the next chapter,
Adopting a Cat. Bear in mind that a pure-bred cat will be a more expensive acquisition and might have more stringent care requirements,
depending on the breed. Also, because of the small pool of available
genes, pure-bred animals can sometimes be more susceptible to hereditary conditions, birth defects, and illness.

So do you have a favorite cat breed you're interested in adopting—
or that you already share your home with? And how much do you

really know about the cat breed you're interested in? Take the following quiz to find out!

CAT FACT

Cats can get pimples. To diminish kitty acne, feed and water your cat from glass or steel bowls as plastic is notorious for harboring blemish-causing germs.

QUIZ #3

Match the description of common characteristics to the breed to which they belong to see how breed savvy you really are.

Cat Breeds

a. American Short Hair

b. Maine Coon

c. Persian

d. Siamese

e. Russian Blue

f. Abyssinian

g. Balinese

h. Egyptian Mau

i. Manx

j. Ocicat

k. Siberian

l. Sphynx

Breed Characteristics

1. This cat's name comes from the Egyptian word for cat. (Want to cheat? Sneak ahead and take a look at "Cat Facts: A Cat By Any Other Name . . ." on page 25.) Sporting a spotted coat—almost like a cheetah—this breed is very intelligent and highly devoted to human companions.

2. This cat breed is among the most unusual of cat breeds: it's completely hairless, with the exception of peach fuzz that softens its skin. Popularized as the pet cat of Dr. Evil in the *Austin Powers* films, this breed is relatively new on the scene: The first were born in Canada in 1978.

3. This breed, available in a wide range of colors and patterns, has one very distinct feature that sets it apart from other cats. It has no tail! Smart, easygoing, and affectionate, this breed makes a great family pet.

4. The only cat indigenous to North America, this sometimes clumsy, horizontally oriented breed is much larger than most other breeds. Males have been known to weigh in at upward of twenty-five pounds—and that's not because they're fat! Docile and friendly, this cat is great with families and even dogs.

5. As the most common North American cat, this breed is the most recognizable. Its short hair can come in any number of patterns and colors. While it makes a great pet, it's much more independent than other breeds and not as affectionate as most other cats.

6. Hailing from Africa, this human-adoring cat has a long, lean body. Playful, verging on zany, and affectionate, its coat is usually cinnamon-colored but also comes in red and blue.

7. Distinct with its vibrant blue eyes and angular features, this cat breed is highly intelligent and demands continuous human doting. Its body fur is usually light, whereas its ears, paws, and tail tip fur are darker.

8. Descended from cats originally from Iran, this long-haired breed is typically not as chatty as many other breeds. Its long coat comes in many colors, but it is most distinct for its face, which looks "shmushed."

9. Emerging on the scene in the 1960s as a combination of Siamese, Abyssinian, and American shorthair breeds, this cat is quite rare and very expensive, but it is very docile and easily trained.

10. The national cat of Russia, this cat was first imported in 1990 and is very rare in the United States. With characteristics that mimic both Siamese and Persians, this long-haired breed is extremely agile and exceptionally curious.

11. This breed has a silvery-blue, plush double coat that has been compared to the fur of a seal or beaver. Gentle, affectionate, and highly entertaining, they get along exceptionally well with small children and other pets.

12. This is a very friendly and playful breed with a particularly loud yowl. Here's a big hint: It is commonly known as a long-haired version of the Siamese cat. And here's another: It is also so close to the Javanese that usually breeders consider these one in the same.

Answers to Quiz #3

1. H. Egyptian Mau.

2. L. Sphynx.

3. I. Manx.

4. B. Maine Coon.

5. A. American Short Hair.

6. F. Abyssinian.

7. D. Siamese.

8. C. Persian.

9. J. Ocicat.

10. K. Siberian.

11. E. Russian Blue.

12. G. Balinese.

Give yourself a point for every correct answer. SCORE:_____

Now turn to page 217 to record your score, then head to the next quiz.

4

Adopting a Cat

The naming of cats is a difficult matter. It isn't just one
of your holiday games. You may think at first I'm mad as
a hatter. When I tell you a cat must have three different
names . . .
—T.S. Eliot, *Old Possum's Book of Practical Cats*

Sure, you like cats, so of course you want to add as many as you can to your life. Perhaps you grew up with a favorite pet kitty—or several—and you haven't had one for years. Or maybe you already have one—or several—and you just can't get enough of these fabulous fur balls.

Whatever your current cat status, if you are ready to bring a new cat into your life, chances are you've already considered all the ways this precious purr-machine is going to change things. Right? Well, if you haven't, here are the biggies:

- You'll be responsible for making sure she is fed and watered properly.
- You will be responsible for making sure she's groomed, that her claws are trimmed, that her ears are clean.
- You will be responsible for making sure she is in purr-fect health—that all her vaccinations are up-to-date, that she sees her vet at least once a year for a checkup.
- But more than anything else, you will be responsible for giving your new friend all the love in the world.

Once you decide you'd like to have a new cat in your life, there are lots of ways to make it happen. For instance, if you have a penchant for a particular type of cat, you can seek one out from a breeder. Remember that you will have to pay for the privilege, and depending on what kind of cat you want to adopt, you could be paying a lot. You can also purchase a cat from a pet store, but the overall health and emotional fitness of pet store cats can be touch and go, so it is not a recommended option.

If it doesn't matter to you whether you new cat is properly pedigreed, keep in mind that there are many cats in shelters that desperately need loving homes. Typically when you adopt a cat from a shelter, they will request a nominal donation to cover the cost of altering the cat and vaccinations.

It might be that there's a certain stray who hangs around your house whom you'd like to adopt. If that's the case, you'll need to proceed with caution. For one, she will likely be especially skittish around humans. Also, there's no guarantee she's had any inoculations. If you have other pets, you're best keeping your new addition away from them until she's received a clean bill of health from your vet, who will test her for various infectious viral and parasitic diseases.

So you think you know something about adopting a cat? Okay, so take the following quiz to see how much you really know.

CAT FACT

Your cat drops his toys in his water bowl and hides food under the couch to protect his stuff from other cats in the house—and that includes you!

QUIZ #4

Answer the following questions True or False to see what you know about bringing a cat into your life.

1. Taking in a stray is the best adoption option.

2. All strays are looking to live in loving homes with doting humans.

3. A breeder will not give you a newborn kitten, no matter how much you want one.

4. Pure breeds are typically the healthiest types of cats.

5. A breeder will spay or neuter a kitten before adopting it out.

6. You can adopt a retired queen or stud from a breeder at a reduced rate.

7. If you can't adopt a stray who hangs around your house, you should ignore him so he'll go away and find someone who does want to adopt him.

8. If you can't make a lifetime commitment, you can become a foster mom or dad to a cat or kitten in need.

9. Most animal shelters have a "no kill" policy.

10. An animal shelter will interview and screen you to ensure you will provide the best possible home for a cat you want to adopt.

Answers to Quiz #4

1. False. While taking in a stray is certainly a noble option, there are many special considerations with which you need to contend when walking down this road. For one, most strays have been just that their entire lives. There's an old saying: You can take the stray

off the street, but you can't take the street out of the stray. It's likely she's been fighting her whole life to survive, and she's not going to shed that instinct like a winter coat when you take her in. Especially if you have small children or other pets, you may want to consider adopting a cat that has had at least some screening.

2. False. This ties in to the previous question. While most can't resist the idea of regular meals, warm, dry shelter, and human companionship, many will fight to get out if made to stay inside. One of the main issues adopters of stray cats face is litter training. Not accustomed to using a "box," to do their business, they are sometimes harder to litter train than kittens. We'll talk more about litter training in chapter 15.

3. True. This is absolutely the case, and if you find a breeder who will, run the other way. That is not a reputable breeder, but a guy trying to make a quick buck who doesn't give a hairball about the cats in his care or what becomes of them. Any good breeder knows that to be physically and emotionally healthy in her life, a kitten needs to stay with her mother at least six to eight weeks after she's born.

4. False. You would think that with all the care that goes into raising them that these cats would always be of exceptional health, but the issues really lie beyond the breeder's control. Essentially, it's a question of genetics. Because they don't have a diverse pool of genes, they are more likely to pass down undesirable traits from generation to generation. So, while perhaps not the most elite choice, a "mutt" cat, complete with a vast mix of genes from God only knows where, is typically more sturdy than a pure-bred cat.

5. True. A good breeder will typically ensure everything is in order before releasing a kitten from his care, and that includes vaccinations and spaying or neutering the cat. Depending on how early you'd like to adopt a cat, however, the business of altering may be left to you. And of course, if you are interested in breeding, you can request the kitten not be altered.

6. True. Most breeders employ their queens for only a few years before it's time to retire them. And while many breeders grow attached to their cats, it is sometimes impossible to provide a loving home for all of them. For that reason, they will seek out loving homes for them. Just be warned: You will likely be carefully screened by the breeder to see if you are qualified to adopt one of her precious animals. Don't be annoyed by this as it is a very good thing. If a breeder is so concerned about what will happen to her animal once it is released into someone else's custody, just imagine how well she treated this cat when it was in hers.

7. False. Aside from being a kind of cruel method to get the animal to go away, no cat lover in his or her right heart would ever be able to resist a mewing stray needing help. Even if you can't adopt her, you can help her—and by that we don't mean simply feeding her. The best way to help her is to "trap" her and take her to a shelter, where she can have a physical exam to make sure she's in good health, as well as be vaccinated and altered. You can always set her free after the procedure, or leave her with the shelter where she'll have a much better chance of getting adopted into a loving home.

8. True. Thankfully, some smart people have realized that shelter overcrowding means less care for the animals therein and a higher chance of having to put these animals down—and they don't like it. So, instead of keeping a cat in a shelter, she is placed in a loving "foster home" on a temporary basis until she can be permanently adopted. In many communities, the option to become a "foster parent" to a cat in need has become a viable solution. If you are inter-

ested in becoming a foster parent to a cat in need, ask your veterinarian or contact your local animal shelter. If they don t have a pro-
gram in place, why not suggest they start one—or help start one
yourself?

9. False. Sorry to have to break this to you, but most animal shelters can't accommodate all the animals that come to them. Sadly,
this means that many shelter animals who are not adopted in a certain time period are put down. Did we mention that one of the best
ways to acquire a new feline friend was through a shelter? This is
the biggest reason why. And not to mention that the shelter will take
care of administering any vaccinations the cat needs and also spay
or neuter the animal before handing it over.

10. True. As much as animal shelters want to have all their animals
adopted and as quickly as possible, they will not adopt animals out
to just anyone. Unfortunately, as shelter employees are well aware,
there are people who are cruel to animals and who are looking for
their latest victims, and then there are those who simply will not be
able to provide a safe and happy environment for an animal. So be
patient with the screening process and remember, it's in the cat's
best interest. If you are a caring and responsible human, you'll be
able to take her home and start loving her and spoiling her soon
enough!

Give yourself a point for every correct answer. SCORE:_____

Now turn to page 217 to record your score, then head to the next quiz.

A CAT BY ANY OTHER NAME . . .

Cats are as worldly as they are mysterious. Just about every country across the globe recognizes the domestic cat as a much sought-after house pet, and each has its own name for the favored feline. Do you know all the terms used throughout the world for "cat?" Here are just a few:

Language	Translation	Language	Translation
Arabic	Biss	Italian	Gatto
Armenian	Gatz	Japanese	Nekko
Bulgarian	Kotka	Latin	Cattus
Chinese	Mio	Maltese	Gattus
Dutch	Kat	Polish	Kot
Egyptian	Mau	Russian	Koskha
Finnish	Kissa	Spanish	Gato
French	Chat	Swahili	Paka
German	Katze	Swedish	Katt
Greek	Catta	Thai	Meo
Hawiian	Popoki	Turkish	Kedi
Hindu	Katas	Ukranian	Kotuk
Icelandic	Kottur	Yiddish	Kats
Indonesia	Qitta		

Source: Cats'n'Kittens, www.cats.alpha.p1

5

Kittens

The smallest feline is a masterpiece.
— Leonardo da Vinci

I n the modern world, we learn more and more that da Vinci was on
to lots of other things besides painting, but who better than da Vinci
is there to define what makes a masterpiece? Da Vinci was a self-
professed cat lover, and like the rest of us, he knew how wondrous the
species is — especially when it comes to kittens.

Let's talk seriously here: Is there anything in the world more cute
than a kitten? Their eyes take up most of their faces. Their bodies have
yet to grow into their giant ears and paws. And of course, they need to
know everything. One minute, they'll dopily dote on you, and the next
they'll shoot off, tracking down some renegade something or other that
has somehow completely eluded everyone else in the room.

The most emphatic cat lover might even profess that a kitten is even
sweeter looking than a new baby, but whether you favor human infants
or their feline counterparts, one thing remains the same with both:
They require lots and lots of care and work. A mother cat, if she is kept
with her kittens, will cover most of the early nurturing by herself. This
is one of the main reasons a kitten should not be taken away from her
mother too early. Does your cat knead on your stomach or on the blan-
kets or pillow of your bed? If she does, this is a sign she was separated
from her mother when she was much too young. The kneading is rem-
iniscent of a kitten's interaction with her mama: as a little one, she

would make this kneading motion on her mother's underbelly to stimulate milk production for her next meal. (As a side note, vaccinations should be given to a new kitten just after she is weaned from her mother because by that point, the immunities the mother has passed through nursing have started to wane.)

If the mother cannot care for her own kittens, humans have been known to rise to the occasion and fill a mother cat's enormous paws. Make no mistake about it: It is a Herculean task. New kittens need to be bottle-fed a special kitten formula several times a day. They also need to be taught to clean themselves and to use a litter box. Eventually, they can be taught to eat solid food, at which time they can be adopted, inevitably breaking the hearts of the surrogates who have invested so much time in their care but who, above all, want nothing more than to have their "babies" placed in loving homes.

How much do you know about kittens and the special care they require? Take the following quiz to find out!

 CAT FACT

In nature, a mother cat introduces solid food to her kittens when they are about four weeks old.

QUIZ #5

Answer the following questions True or False to see if you're ready to *ten into your life.*

1. When a kitten is born, she can see and hear pe

2. The sooner a kitten is separated from he mates, the more social she will be with b

3. You should always keep kittens isol preferably until they reach adultho

4. A kitten can sleep sixteen hours a day.

5. You should develop good habits in your kitten right away. Establish grooming rituals, good eating habits, and behavioral expectations from the day you take her home.

6. A kitten does not instinctively know how to use her litter box.

7. If a kitten has an "accident" when you bring her home, the best way to ensure that she won't do it again is to push her nose in the mess.

8. It takes a year for a kitten to reach sexual maturity.

9. Kittens and human infants typically become fast friends.

10. It's a good idea to teach your kitten to appreciate and crave going out in the big outdoors.

Answers to Quiz #5

1. False. You would think that an animal so revered for its exceptional vision and hearing would be building these skills even in utero, but no. When a kitten is born, he's both deaf and blind. At first, he will just barely look feline and more like a small rodent with ears down and eyes squinched shut. Within a week, his eyes will open, and he will be able to see. Then within two weeks, his hearing will finally develop properly.

2. False. Actually, it's from her early exposure to her littermates that a kitten learns social behavior. A kitten who's learned to get along with her siblings will be more likely to get along with other cats, as well as other animals and humans as she grows into a cat.

3. False. As it works with her littermates, so it works with humans: Kittens need exposure to others to socialize with and get used to them. A kitten who never sees another human aside from his "parents" will be timid and scared around other humans. Imagine if a kitten has been cared for by a small, quiet woman who keeps the kitten sequestered from guests, and then all of a sudden, this woman marries a large, loud, rough man. Just think of how terrifying this behemoth will be to the little one! And that also goes for exposure to children—but we'll get into that more a little later on.

4. True. Sure, a newborn kitten can a sleep sixteen plus hours a day, but never in a row! Sleep usually comes in spurts of naps—minutes in length. But a kitten needs this sleep more than you may realize. As is true with all living things, in sleep, there is growth. From the time she is born to the time she reaches adulthood, a kitten will grow in size from just a few ounces to about eight or more pounds. So as cute as she looks when she's asleep, try not to disturb your kitten. She needs all that rest. And don't worry, without a doubt she'll be up and running around—and tiring herself out again—soon enough!

5. True. Absolutely true. Raising a kitten is a lot like raising a child. She will look to you for cues on how to behave—and she will try and push her boundaries as much as she can. Be consistent yet gentle with her and she will learn right from wrong.

6. True. While feral cats in the wild instinctively bury their urine and feces in dirt and leaves to hide their scent from possible predators, chances are your house is not decorated with forest-like floor treatments. It's more likely that you have a litter box somewhere. How do you teach a kitten to use a litter box? Put her in it several times a day. Every time you think about it, put the kitten in the box. Within a day, her instincts should kick in and adapt to the circumstances.

7. False. The only result you can hope to achieve by forcing your kitten's nose into her own mess is a confused and possibly irate kitten. When you first bring her home, it's likely she'll go somewhere that isn't the litter box. This is pretty normal. The stress of getting acclimated to new surroundings, people, and all those new scents can be very overwhelming for a little one. So if she soils outside the box, remind her where her box is by placing her there right afterward—and several times over the course of the day. Be sure to thoroughly clean the mess, ideally with a cleanser specifically designed to remove cat odors. You don't want her to sniff out the area again and repeat the same boo-boo. Do not use any cleaner with ammonia for this, however. Urine breaks down into ammonia eventually and the scent lingers. For that reason, this type of product will only attract the kitten to the area more.

8. False. Both male and female kittens can begin to show signs of sexual maturity as early as four months, but typically it comes around six months. For that reason, you ideally want to spay or neuter your kitten at about six months. A kitten who goes unaltered will possibly drive both you and herself nuts by exhibiting wild, rambunctious behavior, possibly wrecking your home by constantly knocking things over, and may even start spraying urine to put his or her scent out for a potential mate.

9. False. Unfortunately—or perhaps it's more fortunately—kittens are not big fans of infants, who are perceived by your constancy-loving kitty as erratic, crazy cry balls. So while it might be disappointing that your kitten won't dote on your baby, don't worry: as they each get older, they'll likely get used to one another.

10. False. Fresh air aside, there are not that many good reasons to bring a kitten outdoors and let her roam around freely. Indoor cats live significantly longer than outdoor cats (see page 205), so you want your cat to be indoors-oriented. That doesn't mean a kitten shouldn't be able to enjoy the outdoors, however. Why not create a perch for her by a window so she can safely watch the action in complete comfort?

Give yourself a point for every correct answer. SCORE:_____

Now turn to page 217 to record your score, then head to the next quiz.

6
Famous Film and TV Felines

You can fool everybody, but landie dearie me, you can't
fool a cat. They seem to know who's not right.
—Woman at pet shop, *Cat People* (1942)

A nyone knows that what makes a *good* television show or movie *great* is the casting of a smart, charismatic cat who carries the production with effortless grace. And whether these cats gift the production with their presence as actors—or silent directors—cats have always made for indispensable muses for creative people. Feline antics simply inspire creative thought. Aldous Huxley once wrote: "If you want to be a psychological novelist and write about human beings, the best thing you can do is keep a pair of cats." Don't believe it? Just think of all the movies made with cats in mind: *Cat Woman* (2004), *Cat Girl* (1957), *Cat People* (1942 and 1982), *The Black Cat* (1941 and 1961), *Cat's Eye* (1985), and so many more.

The most famous TV cats are so popular, they're iconic. The finicky face of Morris the cat has become synonymous with Nine Lives cat food. And what about that preciously prissy Persian who eats her Fancy Feast from a lead crystal dessert dish?

Of course, if you're thinking your cat oughta be in pictures, you might want to think again. It's not that cats aren't smart—in fact, they are very smart. Most cats don't particularly like acting because it means they have to do someone else's bidding. Follow orders? Are you kidding! Still, some love the idea of being in the spotlight, and for a tasty reward, will humor the humans, at least for a while. As we'll see in the next section, it's not impossible to train a cat. You just have to know the terms.

So how much do you know about film and TV kitties? Take the following quiz to see.

CAT FACT
Cats really like carbonation, so why not try adding a little club soda to ordinary water as a special treat!

QUIZ #6

Are you a true fan of feline films and TV shows? Match up the cat with the TV show or film to see what you really know.

1. Salem
2. Church
3. Fat Louie
4. Azrael
5. Snowball
6. Duchess
7. Sylvester
8. Syn
9. Puss-Puss
10. Mr. Tinkles
11. Sassy
12. Sebastian

a. *The Smurfs*
b. *The Simpsons*
c. *The Princess Diaries*
d. *The Aristocats*
e. *That Darn Cat*
f. *Sabrina the Teenage Witch*
g. *Pet Sematary*
h. *Looney Tunes*
i. *Kid Notorious*
j. *Josie and the Pussycats*
k. *Homeward Bound: The Incredible Journey*
l. *Cats and Dogs*

Answers to Quiz #6

1. F. His full name is Salem Saberhagen and he is actually a warlock who's been transformed into a cat on *Sabrina the Teenage Witch*. In the show, a real black cat played some of Salem's scenes, while a puppet was used for the talking sequences.

2. G. Possibly one of the scariest cats in the history of cinema, Church was the Creed family cat in *Pet Sematary*—until an unfortunate accident with a truck ended his life. To shield the family from the loss, dad Louis Creed buries Church in a haunted pet cemetery. When Church comes back from the dead, the tagline "Sometimes dead is better" really starts to make sense!

3. C. What cat's been luckier than *The Princess Diaries'* Fat Louie? One day, he's living in a dilapidated San Francisco loft with his good friend Mia and her mom, and the next thing he knows, he's living as royalty in a palace in a small European country. Way to pick a human, Louie!

4. A. The wizard Gargamel's orange cat, Azrael, had a real appetite for the little blue creatures that live in the forest, but he unfortunately was never able to dine on any of those tasty *Smurfs*.

5. B. In the now-sixteen-year run of *The Simpsons*, there have actually been two Snowballs. Sadly, the first one was run over by a car early on in the show, so the one who buddies around with Santa's Little Helper now is actually Snowball II.

6. D. Duchess and her kittens inherited a huge fortune from their human in the 1970 Disney classic, *The Aristocats*.
    Bonus point: Which actress supplied the voice of Duchess? (ans: Eva Gabor)

7. H. As everyone's favorite cat with a speech impediment, Sylvester first joined the Looney Tunes cast in the 1940s. And, "sufferin' succotash," even about sixty years later, he has yet to dine on his much-sought meal of Tweety Bird.

8. E. *That Darn Cat* Syn holds the key (or collar) to solving a kidnapping, working first with Haley Mills in 1965 and then Christina Ricci in 1997.

9. I. Robert Evans's cartoon self hardly goes anywhere without his femme fatale, golden-eyed, all-black kitten Puss-Puss in Comedy Central's *Kid Notorious*.

10. L. Mr. Tinkles is the ruthless white Persian who carefully plots the demise of all canines in *Cats and Dogs* (2001).
 Bonus point: Which actor supplied the voice of Mr. Tinkles? (ans: Sean Hayes)

11. K. Haughty Himalayan Sassy joins her family's two dogs in a quest to get back to their family in 1993s *Homeward Bound: The Incredible Journey*.
Bonus point: Which actress supplied the voice of Sassy? (ans: Sally Field)

12. J. Black with a white streak in his fur, just like his human, Alexandra Cabot, Sebastian was the only true cat in the 1970s cartoon *Josie and the Pussycats*.

Give yourself a point for every correct answer, plus an extra point for each bonus question you answered correctly. SCORE:_____

Now turn to page 217 to record your score, then head to the next quiz.

7

Training Your Cat

*Of all God's creatures, there is only one that cannot be
made slave of the leash. That one is the cat.*
—Mark Twain

Training a cat? Does such a phenomenon actually exist? Believe it or not, the answer is yes. But don't get the wrong idea here about what it actually means to train a cat. Your feline friend will only tolerate a certain amount of commands—if any at all. If you want a pet to perform parlor tricks on demand, you're probably better off getting a dog.

Training a cat is essential. There are certain, basic, and fundamental things you want your cat to be able to do. You want her to be able to find her food and water, to use her litter box correctly. Then there are other things that make her a welcome and functional member of the household, such as staying off of countertops, avoiding the furniture when the scratching urge arises, and not nipping at the fingers or toes of small children. You also want to establish behaviors that promote safety, like teaching her not to chew on electrical wires or jump into the refrigerator or oven before she has to find out the hard way by herself that these are all terrible ideas.

Keep in mind: There are some things you will never be able to train your cat to do. For example, she will never fetch your slippers—though she might run off with your dirty socks and hide them under the bed or somewhere else you may never expect or be able to find.

So how much do you know about the art of training a cat? Take the next quiz to see.

CAT FACT

Training your cat strengthens the bond between the two of you.

QUIZ #7

What do you know about training a cat? Answer the following questions True or False to find out.

1. You can raise your cat's IQ by training him.

2. Cats are completely true to their reputation of being indomitable; they will not let you train them if they don't wish to be trained.

3. A cat can be trained to shake hands.

4. It's in a cat's instinctual makeup to beg; unfortunately, if she's a begger, she cannot be taught otherwise.

5. A cat can be taught to walk on a leash.

6. A cat can be trained to meow on command.

7. You can train your cat to come to you when you call him.

8. If a cat has decided he wants to be somewhere you don't want him to be, he will likely never learn to comply with your wishes.

9. The best way to discipline your cat is to give him a light slap on his hindquarters when he misbehaves.

10. The most sought-after reward a cat will work for is a loving pat on the head from his favorite human.

Answers to Quiz #7

1. True. Studies have shown that training a cat is a great way for him to learn. And just like humans, the more he knows, the smarter he will become.

2. False. While you can't force a cat to do anything he doesn't want to do, he won't mind doing things that he gets rewarded to do. Whether this reward takes the form of a loving pat or even a cat treat—preferably the latter—he will enjoy the positive reinforcement and most likely act to have it repeated as often as possible.

3. True. It's a common belief that a cat would never deign to dirty his paw by shaking a human hand (that's the dog's job), but most cats can easily be trained to shake hands—and some more easily than their canine counterparts. To teach your cat to shake your hand, sit in front of him. Tap his paw with your hand and say "shake." He will react by trying to pull his paw away, at which point you should lightly shake it. When you do, be sure to give him happy, gentle, verbal approval, a loving pat with your free hand, and even a cat treat.

4. False. Sometimes in the morning, a cat can howl so loudly and emphatically that her human might panic, wondering if she has forgotten to feed her feisty fur ball for a couple of days. Don't panic: Your cat would never allow you to forget a meal. Just keep in mind that cats are very manipulative creatures. Your cat knows how to work you, and if you've succumbed to her cries for food or light slaps with her paw in the wee hours of the morning, she will continue to use this method with you. She's not ever going to feel sorry for you: Only you can put a stop to it. The best way to make her stop is to just ignore her. Eventually, she will get bored and decide it's time for a new strategy. If, however, you have an exceptionally tenacious tabby, you might have to confine her a few nights to a room situated as far away from the bedroom as possible. She will not starve to death, but she will learn that you're not the pushover she may have had you pegged for.

Another method is to push the time back slowly, about half an hour at a time, until your cat is finally eating when you want her to.

5 True. Yes, your cat can be taught to walk on a leash—though this doesn't mean that he'll necessarily like it. And with most any training exercise, the best time to train a cat to walk on a leash is when he's a kitten. Walking a cat on a leash may seem a little strange, but it's actually a great way to let your cat experience a bit of the outdoors safely as well as a great workout for a flabby feline. Keep in mind that just because you *can* teach your cat to walk on a leash doesn't necessarily mean that you *should*; it may be something he profoundly dislikes, and something that will cause a rift between the two of you. So see how it goes. If it's not going to happen, there are plenty of exercise alternatives that we'll discover later in this book.

6. True. Yes, as every cat owner knows, you *can* train your cat to meow on command. But that doesn't mean it's particularly nice to do. While you may enjoy listening to your frustrated cat run through all her available octaves as you dangle her food bowl over her head, just out of her reach, just remember that she's not enjoying having to perform for you.

7. False. It doesn't matter what you have to offer her as a reward for coming to you because *you* feel like visiting with her. A cat does not want to come to you just because you want her to. Now, if you call her and she thinks, "Hey, I haven't seen that guy in a while. I think I'll go see what he's up to," then yeah, she'll come to you. But if she wants to be left alone, that's what's going to happen. Don't believe us? Try it. Make a note the next ten times you call your cat and see how many of those times she comes to you. And no cheating: Be sure she's been fed first. It's only fair. You may be surprised to see the number won't be as high as you think it will be.

8. False. While cats can get very interested and drawn to places they want to be, there are ways of changing their minds: You simply have to make the visit to the desired locale less pleasant than your cat will be counting on it to be. A great way to get a cat to not jump all over your countertop, for example, is to stretch a layer of aluminum foil across the surface. You won't have to keep it there for very long. Cats actually hate the crinkly feel of the foil under their feet and will avoid the sensation at all costs.

9. False. You should never slap, hit, punch, or kick your cat—or any animal for that matter. Slapping a cat is not an effective way to discipline him. The cat will not associate the slap with the action, and it will only make him harbor resentment against you. One discipline tool people use for their cats is a spray bottle filled with water, like the kind you use to spray your plants, or even a water gun. Cats are not typically fans of water, but more than that, they absolutely hate surprises. This could have negative ramifications, however. Your cat could actually start resenting you for it. Another method people use to keep cats away from places they should not be is to stack a tower of paper cups around the area. If she knocks over the tower, she will be startled, and the chances are fairly certain that she will not be repeating whatever it was that startled her so any time soon.

10. False. While it's nice to dream that your cat can be motivated by affection alone, believing this to be true is pure folly. It's not that your cat doesn't love *you*; it's just that your cat *really* loves food. A lot. In fact, she will do just about anything you want her to for food. If she could add, she'd probably even do your taxes for a tasty treat.

Give yourself a point for every correct answer. SCORE:_____

Now turn to page 217 to record your score, then head to the next quiz.

8

Cat-Proofing Your Home

After scolding one's cat one looks into its face and is seized
by the ugly suspicion that it understood every word. And
has filed it for reference.
—Charlotte Gray

D o you really need to cat-proof your home? The answer is a re-
sounding yes. The phrase "curiosity killed the cat" did not
just pop out of the sky. As you well know, your cat is the most curious and inquisitive of creatures. He is also something of a creative
genius, inventing new toys out of any number of basic household
items. The problem is, not all of these items will be particularly safe
for him to play with; nor will every substance he sniffs or licks be
free of harmful ramifications. And not to mention you may have
things you'd rather your cat did not touch.

For these reasons and more, it's essential to make sure your
home is cat-proofed before bringing one of these lovable creatures
into your domain. Think of your cat as a toddler—except with the
ability to outrun you and jump to incredible heights and hide in
places in which no human being could ever even dream of squeez-
ing into. For your cat's health and sanity—not to mention yours—
take the proper precautions before finding out the hard way what
your cat is capable of and what could be dangerous and even lethal
to him.

Think you know all about what it takes to cat-proof your home?
Take the next quiz to see.

CAT FACT

Want to keep your cat off your wood furniture? Polish it often! Most cats dislike citrus-smelling furniture polish.

QUIZ #8

Has your house been properly cat-proofed? Answer the following statements True or False to see.

1. Cats are not interested in shiny metal objects, so it's okay to leave your wedding band on your bedside table if you need to take it off at night.

2. Your cat loves azaleas as much as you do, so it's a good idea to keep bouquets of them within easy sniffing distance for your cat.

3. Your insatiably curious cat wants to know what everything is, and will attempt to sniff everything in her domain. For that reason, you should keep all cleansers and other chemicals in well-secured cabinets.

4. Ribbons and rubber bands make for dangerous cat toys.

5. Your cat knows better than to stick a paw in an electrical outlet.

6. It's funny when my cat climbs up the strings for the blinds. She's so rambunctious, she sometimes gets herself all caught up in them.

7. Tylenol can be lethal for cats.

8. If you have a prized possession that is fragile and you leave it out and unprotected, your cat might break it.

9. Your cat fully understands the concept of a window screen and will not try to push through one—no matter how delectable a bird or squirrel she spots outside.

10. Even if they are not plugged into anything, electrical cords make terrible toys for cats.

Answers to Quiz #8

1. False. Cats love shiny metal objects. They love to bat them around and they love to swallow them. Doesn't your cat play the "gravity game"? When she sees something cluttering up a surface, does she not feel irresistibly compelled to knock it off? That's the least of the trouble here: She might also feel compelled to swallow it, which could lead to a dangerous intestinal blockage. So unless you want to make a visit to the vet that might mean surgery or go digging through your cat's litter for your wedding ring, always put it out of reach of kitty's playful paw.

2. False. While she might be drawn to the lovely bright blooms, these, and many other flowers, are quite toxic to your cat and should therefore be put well out of your cat's reach—and jumping distance—if you even keep them in your house at all. See page 108 for more potentially hazardous cat toxins.

3. True. Your cat will not be able to tell the difference between iced tea and Pine-Sol unless she has a chance to sniff both out for herself. And she does want to know the difference—believe us. Unfortunately, her investigation of harmful chemicals might lead to a spilled container and possible ingestion, which is a very bad thing. Keep cabinets secure at all times. If your cat does

manage to get in and swallow anything, call the Animal Poison Control Center hotline immediately at 1-888-426-4435.

4. True. While your cat may love the feeling of satin ribbon on her tongue or the delight she derives from chewing on a stretchy rubber band, these are potentially dangerous for her, sometimes causing intestinal blockage if swallowed. Some cats know better than to swallow ribbon, and they simply enjoy licking the satiny surface, but do you really want to take the chance that your cat won't try to eat it? And that goes for any kind of string or anything string-like, which could also cause an obstruction that can only be cleared up through surgery.

5. False. Your cat is curious about everything, and until she is shown differently, will think just about anything in the home is safe for exploration. To avoid having your kitty electrify herself, insert those plastic child-proof outlet guards in any electrical outlet that is currently not in use.

6. False. True, your cat's antics can be hilarious, but not when they happen at the expense of his safety. Strings that dangle from vertical or horizontal blinds can be treacherous for cats. Imagine your kitty getting tangled up in them when you aren't home to free him. He could strangle himself. Not so funny anymore. For that reason, you should keep the strings for your blinds securely fastened—perhaps wrapped around small hooks you can easily install in your wall.

7. True. Most human medications can be toxic to cats. Swallowing just one Tylenol could even prove fatal for a kitten. For this reason, just as you keep cleansers securely locked away, so should you keep medications. For more information on things that are toxic to your cat, see page 108.

8. True. Your cat does *not* know the difference between the crystal vase your dear Aunt Helen gave you as a wedding present and a drinking glass you may have picked up at a gas station as a bonus for filling your tank. She will never intentionally knock your valuables over, but in her quest to find the best perch from which to observe the machinations of your household, she might just break a few things so keep valuable objects behind closed doors if possible.

9. False. While your cat will generally be able to sit politely on the inside of a screened-in window, there may come a time that something she sees on the outside will be just be irresistibly pounce-able. She may get so carried away that she will try and push right through the screen. To prevent this from happening, be sure your screens are securely set in your windows. Better yet, keep your cat's favorite windows nearly shut; if they are open only a fraction, your cat won't be able to slip out of them, but she will be able to poke her nose at the screen for a whiff of fresh air. And make sure they are nice and clean and clear so kitty can really enjoy the view!

10. True. Just because there's no electrical circuit running through them does not mean electrical cords are suitable toys for cats. For one, they can cause strangulation. An electrical cord is typically thick and sturdy; a cat can easily get it caught around her throat by scrambling around with it in her mouth. Also, under the plastic coating of these cords lies a network of fine wires. If she bites through the plastic, she could get to the wires, snap them, and easily choke on the pieces. For this reason, electrical cords that are not in use should be stowed securely away.

Give yourself a point for every correct answer. SCORE:_____

Now turn to page 217 to record your score, then head to the next quiz.

One of the best gifts you can give your cat is the gift of good health. To that end, you want to put her in the hands of the best veterinarian possible—someone who's not only well qualified, but who also has a great bedside manner. That's why you need to put more legwork into choosing a vet than simply picking up the Yellow Pages. When trying to decide on a vet for your cat, ask yourself the following questions:

- *Is she conveniently located?* Especially in the case of an emergency, but even if you just need to make a quick stop on your way to work, it's helpful to not have to travel too far to get to your vet.

- *Has she been recommended by friends or neighbors?* All the diplomas in the world mean nothing next to a sound recommendation from someone you know. If your friends and neighbors have good things to say about a vet, you may just want to check her out.

- *Are his offices clean and safely designed?* This seems like common sense, but you'd be surprised what some people try and get away with. If you think the conditions in a vet's office are unseemly, by all means, take your cat somewhere else.

- *Does he know what he's talking about?* You don't have to know that much about veterinary science to figure out whether your vet knows his stuff. If he can't answer basic questions or gives you unsatisfactory information, he's probably not the right vet for you.

- *Does she take your phone calls and is she glad to answer your questions?* If she's not available to you, then what are you paying her for? A good vet knows your cat's health is of the utmost importance to you, and, within reason, should let you know what's going on. We say "within reason" because you should not be harassing your vet all the time. She has other patients after all!

- *Does he offer emergency services?* This can mean life or death for your cat, so if your vet's office does not specifically offer emergency services, he should be able to tell you how and where you can obtain them if God forbid they are ever required.

- *Do you like the people he has on staff and do you feel comfortable with them handling your cat?* You're not always going to be around when your cat is in the care of your vet and his staff, and although you might adore your vet, if you don't like one or more of his assistants, you may want to mention this, or take your cat to a place where the you feel more comfortable with the staff.

- *Are her rates competitive?* Going to the vet can be a pricey endeavor. Today, there is such a thing as pet health insurance, but it's not easy to get for all pets. Your vet should give you an itemized estimate for all services provided and fully explain the necessity of those services. Also, he should offer reasonable alternatives for care if finances are an issue.

- *Do you like him?* If you don't particularly like your vet, you're not going to be in any rush to ensure that your cats see him as often as they should. You don't have to want to hang out with him on weekends—or even write a book with him—but your interactions with him should be as pleasant as possible.

- *Does he like animals?* Seems like a silly question, right? But there are vets who are just doing a job looking after animals. For them, they could be working with cars as easily as pets. Watch your vet interact with your cat. Does he treat her with gentleness and respect, or does he handle her like a box of auto parts. You know what to do if the answer is the latter.

9

Cats in History

Cats are intended to teach us that not everything in nature has a purpose.
—Garrison Keillor

With a couple of dark, grim exceptions, cats have universally been revered as wonderful companions throughout history. Many famous people had a passion and reverence for cats, such as Abraham Lincoln, Sir Winston Churchill, Sir Isaac Newton, Florence Nightingale. Interestingly enough, those with a noted disdain for the noble species include Adolph Hitler, Julius Caesar, and Napolean Bonaparte.

The ancient Egyptians were actually the first culture of record with a reverence for the feline. These people considered their cats to be high-standing members of the household and passionately mourned their passing—sometimes more than their human family members. So high on the pedestal of all things loved were the Egyptians' cats that they actually took precautions to have their furry friends cared for even after their own deaths: One Egyptian sultan was said to have left his entire fortune to the welfare of cats in need.

The Egyptians weren't the only culture to hold their cats in such high regard. In ancient Siam, it has been documented that a cat actually rode in the front chariot in a parade celebrating the coronation of a new king. In the ninth century, King Henry I of Saxony decreed the fine for killing a cat as sixty bushels of corn.

But history has not always been kind to cats. During the Dark

Ages, many were killed under suspicion of being demonic beings. In the darkest possible way, you could say the joke was on civilization at large; with the number of cats significantly decreased, plague-carrying rats thrived and spread disease. The Black Plague, also known as the Black Death, killed more than one-third of the world's known population in three years.

Luckily, cats in the present have, for the most part, come back to a place of reverence and adoration.

How much do you know about cats throughout history? Take the following quiz to see.

CAT FACT
Your cat's night vision is ten times better than yours.

QUIZ #9

Answer the following statements True or False to test your knowledge of cats throughout the ages.

1. Cats have been domesticated for thousands of years.

2. In ancient Egypt, cherished cats were sacrificed to the gods.

3. Embalmed mice were placed in tombs with the mummies of ancient Egyptian cats.

4. The ancient Egyptians were so devoted to their cats, family members shaved off their eyebrows in mourning when their beloved felines passed on.

5. Cats were introduced to Europe by Phoenician tradesmen.

6. Ancient mariners thought of black cats as good-luck charms.

7. Christopher Columbus and his crew first introduced cats to the New World.

8. Cats kept soldiers company in the trenches during World War I.

9. When witches were burned at the stake, their cats were spared as the world finally learned that cats were essential to keep the rat population under control.

10. The life expectancy of the domesticated cat is about the same now as it has always been.

Answers to Quiz #9

1. True. People have been enjoying the companionship of cats since the ancient Egyptians first domesticated the species somewhere around 3000 BCE. This is just about as long as dogs have been household pets.

2. False. While many ancient cultures have been known to sacrifice living things dear to them, including human family members, to show the gods just how devoted they were, cats were never the subjects of any of these sacrifices. In fact, killing a cat in ancient Egypt could earn the transgressor a penalty of death.

3. True. Just as humans were buried in tombs with their prized worldly possessions to be taken into the next life with them, so were cats. In fact, one excavated tomb produced the mummies of more than 300,000 cats and their treats for the afterlife: embalmed mice.

4. True. The devotion of the ancient Egyptians to their cats was not something to be taken lightly. So distraught would a family be when its beloved feline passed on, they would shave off their eyebrows as a show of great mourning—and some would even shave all the hair from their bodies!

5. True. In about 900 BCE, Phoenician tradesmen brought short-haired cats to Italy, and from there, the cat population spread throughout Europe, and eventually the world.

6. False. As it is today so it was then. Black cats were actually considered to be quite unlucky as it was thought that these *chats noir* were responsible for bringing bad weather.

7. False. It was actually the pilgrims in the 1600s who brought the first domesticated cats into North America.

8. True. In addition to providing companionship to World War I soldiers, cats in the trenches waged their own battles: against mice and other vermin.

9. False. No, not even the deaths of roughly 75 million people was enough to convince some that cats were integral to the health and safety of the population. In the fifteenth century, when setting so-called witches aflame was all the rage, Pope Innocent VIII decreed that all "cat worshippers" be burned at the stake along with their "demonic" cats.

10. False. Due to proper medical care, advances in cat nutrition, and more, cats live longer today than ever before. In fact, today the average lifespan of the domesticated cat has doubled from eight in 1930 to about sixteen.

Give yourself a point for every correct answer. SCORE:_____

Now turn to page 217 to record your score, then head to the next quiz.

10

Introducing Another Cat to Your One-Cat Household

I have studied many philosophers and many cats. The wisdom of cats is infinitely superior.
—Hippolyte Taine

Sure, you pay the rent or mortgage. And yes, it's you who has to call the plumber when the toilet's broken. But if you share your living space with a cat, you know very well that it isn't *your* house or apartment where you live: the "owner" of your domicile is your cat. Or at least that's what *he* thinks. Which is why when you want to bring another cat into your home, you need to proceed with much care and caution.

Cats are by nature extremely territorial—some more than others. When a new guy comes in, your cat's territory is threatened, and the reaction is usually adverse. Your cat might hiss at the intruder and in some cases even try to attack it. On the other end of the spectrum, your cat might take the intrusion out on you. A typically loving and friendly cat can become antisocial, despondent, and really whiny. But this reaction is normally only a temporary thing.

While cats do have a reputation for being solitary creatures, this is mostly just part of their mystique. As your cat gets used to the new guy, you might find them wrestling a lot, and even fighting, but eventually, you'll be pleasantly surprised to walk in on them curled up napping together or even grooming one another. But don't expect this kind of acceptance to happen overnight. It sometimes takes days, weeks, and even months for cats to get adjusted to each other.

Of course, sometimes you are going to have two cats that just don't get along and who never will. How can you ensure that your cats will grow to tolerate and even like each other? How much do you know about bringing cats together? Take the following quiz and find out!

CAT FACT
The best time to bring a new kitten home is at the end of the week. That way, you will have the weekend to get to know each other.

QUIZ #10

Answer the following questions True or False, then turn to page 54 to see how you did.

1. The best way to introduce two cats to each other is to stick them in a room together with the door closed.

2. Cats are solitary animals and should never live with other cats.

3. Cats need to establish their own guidelines and parameters when allowing a new cat to come and live in their homes.

4. The ideal companion for your older female cat is an older male cat.

5. The best situation is to introduce two cats to a new home at the same time.

6. When cats fight, most of the time they are just playing.

7. If your cats do start fighting with each other, jump right in there and pull them apart.

8. If you have more than one cat, it helps to give them separate feeding stations.

9. You only need to have one litter box available to your pets when you have two cats.

10. Cats are known to cuddle with and groom other cats they live with.

Answers to Quiz #10

1. False. Maybe the best way to *kill* two cats who don't know one another is to stick them in a room together with the door closed. This type of situation is highly intimidating to your felines and is sure to freak out even the calmest kitty. Work your cats into the introductions slowly. Depending on how skittish the animals are, you'll have to proceed in a couple of different ways. For very nervous kitties, try to isolate the new guy in his own room, with food and water and litter of course, for a few hours—or even a few days. Strange smells can be very upsetting for a cat, so allow the resident cat to sniff at the closed door. When both cats seem calm enough, open the door and let the cats suss each other out, but keep an eye on them. If antagonistic behavior ensues, separate them again. Another option you have for introduction is to bring the new cat out in her carrier and let the two get acquainted through the door. Your cats will let you know which option is best!

2. False. Cats do actually enjoy the company of other cats. When they get used to each other and establish their territory and guidelines, many of them actually become great friends. And in reality, it's much easier to have two cats than it is to have one. For example, if you have to go out of town for a few days, your cats can keep each other company. Also, when they have a playmate with whom to exhaust all the extra energy cats seem to have, they won't take out that energy on your furniture or important papers.

3. True. Never force your cat to interact with the newcomer. When she's ready, she'll welcome the new guy in her own way

4. False. While how cats will get along depends a lot on their individual personalities, some kitty combos are definitely more successful than others. An older female cat is suspicious of strangers to begin with; to bring in a male who will dominate her space will stress her out. Conversely, when you bring an older female into an older male cat's home, she will have a very hard time establishing territory. It isn't an impossible situation, but it's just not an ideal one. What are some of the best combinations for fast friends? An older, neutered male will typically take to either a male or female kitten. It's important to him to remain dominant, so a kitten will not pose a threat to him. For an older female cat, a younger female is best. There may be a little discord at first, but within a week, once the initial threat of newness has gone away, it will be like they've always known each other.

5. True. Ah yes, in a perfect world, two cats will get their new humans and home at the same time and therefore won't have as many jealousy and territory issues. We did say in a perfect world, right?

5. True. Sometimes cats can get in pretty scary tussles. Just as lion cubs wrestle each other in the jungle, so do their domestic counterparts express affection in the same way.

7. False. Actually, the worst thing to do if your cats are caught up in a scuffle is to get in there yourself. Especially if your cats have claws, you may be risking serious injury to yourself. In addition, cats fight to establish dominance. They need to work their stuff out on their own. If you think the fighting is getting too violent and that they are in danger of doing serious harm to each other, try making a loud noise. You might also try tossing something at them—something soft, like a pillow. You don't want to hurt them, you just want to startle them and shake the mood.

8. True. By giving them each a calm respite whereby to enjoy their meals, they won't feel threatened—justified or not—that the other will be eating all their food.

9. False. Cats are by nature highly hygienic animals and they like their spaces to be as clean as they keep themselves. For that reason, you should have as many litter boxes available as you have cats— and even one more if space allows. In addition to cleaner spaces, this also ensures that no one will have to wait for the other to use the box.

10. True. Once cats get accustomed to one another, you'll often find them curled up together. They know this is the best way to get those adorable faces of theirs clean!

Give yourself a point for every correct answer. SCORE:_____

Now turn to page 217 to record your score, then head to the next quiz.

11

Introducing Your Cat to Infants, Children, and Other Pets

*A kitten is so flexible that she is almost double; the hind
parts are equivalent to another kitten with which the
forepart plays. She does not discover that her tail belongs
to her until you tread on it.*
—Henry David Thoreau

When it comes to bringing a new cat into your home, maybe the only thing you have to worry about is that you already have a cat—one who has already established his territory and your place in his life. Or maybe your situation is more complicated. Perhaps you have an infant or small children already living with you—or perhaps there's a baby on the way. Maybe you already have a healthy menagerie of dogs, birds, turtles, or what have you in your home, and introducing a cat into everyones' lives is the final element of your big, happy family equation.

But you don't think it will be that easy. From what you understand about cats, they are hugely territorial and, they don't take well to change. And forget about making new friends: A cat will never be pushed to be best buds with anyone—especially not a screeching baby or a big sloppy dog. But guess what? There may be some things you may not know about cats that will possibly make you let go of any trepidation you have. Sure, cats may be shy at first as they try to get their bearings when you bring them into a new situation, but as soon as they can establish their special place in a family, they typically will fit right in — and, most of the time, will even make an effort at it if need be.

When it comes down to it, cats may be independent spirits, but they are also highly sociable creatures. If there's a party going on, they want to be a part of it. On their own terms, yes, but they like to be included. If there's affection being doled out by the humans, they're going to make darn sure they get their fair share.

Just a side note on this attention business: If you had a cat before you had a baby, try not to neglect him (your cat) too much when the new baby comes along. The stress of losing his mommy or daddy to another is already tough on him; he needs to be reassured sometimes that he is still your special baby and will always be — no matter who else you bring into the home.

So, you think you know all about bringing a cat into an already-hectic household? Take the following quiz to see!

CAT FACT

While some kitties may enjoy being cuddled infant-style, most cats like to be held right side up, with one of your arms underneath to support their weight, and the other holding them close to your chest.

QUIZ #11

Answer the following statements True or False to see if you're ready to introduce a cat to the rest of your family.

1. When you bring a new cat into your home, you should introduce her to the rest of the family right away.

2. Never let your cat near your baby. In fact, if you can manage to hide the baby from the cat, that will be best for everyone involved.

3. Your small children should be permitted to hold your cat.

4. A kitten makes a great gift for a child.

5. Kids can be given chores of looking after your cat, such as feeding and watering and making sure the litter box is clean.

6. Cats and kittens smother babies, mostly out of jealousy.

7. Children should be taught their cat's unique boundaries and be expected not to cross them.

8. To ensure your dog and cat get along with each other, leave them alone together. Let them work out their relationship on their own so they will know how to act around each other when you're not around.

9. Cats and dogs can make for really good friends.

10. Your new cat schemes every day to achieve her heart's desire: to make a meal of your parakeet, hamster, goldfish, or box turtle.

Answers to Quiz #11

1. False. While you want your cat to acclimate to her new surroundings as quickly as possible, you also don't want to completely freak her out. On the other hand, there are ways you absolutely should not handle the situation. For example, you should not shut her off in a closet and have family members enter, shut the door, and introduce themselves. This will likely end badly: The cat, feeling cornered and threatened, may attack her visitors. On the other hand, it may not be a good idea to let her introduce herself to others on her own terms. She might not get to it. What she needs is just a little push. First, let her explore her surroundings for a while and get her bearings; then start the introductions.

2. False. One thing your cat really hates is surprises. If there's a new little someone living with you, she should know about it. We're not saying you should plunk your kitty into your new baby's bassinet with him; this is an introduction you want to make as gradually as possible. As you're setting up the nursery, allow your cat to inspect what you're doing. Even if this room is off-limits to your cat, there's nothing more frustrating for her than to know that there's a room in the house she's been forbidden to explore. Buy some baby lotion, rub it in your hands, and allow your cat to sniff it. And before the baby comes home, Dad should bring home with him an article of clothing with the baby's scent so kitty can get a whiff of that, too. When the baby comes home, let your cat inspect him while you are holding him. She will be curious about him—she can't help herself—so let her get acquainted while you're around. While they may not be best friends right away, or even for several years, they'll at least start developing their relationship together.

3. True. If you forbid your child to hold your cat or kitten, chances are she will try and grab a hold of Tiger herself. And that could get ugly. Allow her to hold the cat when Mommy or Daddy is present. Be sure she is sitting down and instruct her how to hold her arms. Then you should pick up the cat or kitten and gently place him in your child's arms. If he squirms away, don't force him to stay. You'll only agitate him and your child could end up with a nasty scratch. Simply let him go and try again later.

4. False. Though it's adorable to think of your child growing up side by side with a new kitten, children and kittens do not make for the best playmates. A child may not know his own strength, and in wanting the kitten to be near him whenever possible, he might accidentally hurt the little fragile cat-to-be. Your best bet is to start your child out with an older cat.

5. True. Of course, that doesn't mean that your three-year-old will be up to the task. You need to wait a bit longer than that—perhaps when the child is of school age and is already beginning to hone her sense of responsibility through homework assignments and such. But even then, you must monitor your child as she completes her tasks; you don't want kitty to starve to death or dehydrate or soil all over the house because there's no room for any more waste in her overflowing box. There are at least a couple—and many more—reasons why gradually handing over cat duties to your little one is a really good idea. On top of the obvious glee you will feel at being free from having to scoop a cat box, your child, as she is learning what it means to be responsible for another living creature, will also develop a deep bond with the cat—and the cat with your child.

6. False. Is your biggest fear the old wives' tale that your cat will become ominously jealous of the little one taking up all your time and attention and smother your baby while she sleeps? Rest easy: This is a myth. Cats typically avoid infants as much as they can. Most cats dislike being around babies altogether as the eardrum-shattering noise and erratic activity levels of the typical human infant make cats really uneasy. Still, you always want to keep your cat–infant visits supervised. Just because your cat won't act out of malice doesn't mean she won't be startled by the screeching and gurgling new creature. You don't want her to accidentally scratch or bite your little one out of fear.

7. True. Everyone in your household deserves to have their boundaries respected, and that includes your cat. Children may have a tendency to get overzealous when it comes to hanging out with their furry friends, and your cat may become nervous or even agitated if she doesn't have any peace or privacy. Remind your child that when your cat is eating or drinking, sleeping, using the litter box, or even hiding under the bed or in a closet, she is not to be disturbed—and enforce this rule consistently.

8. False. While the cartoons give an exaggerated picture of what happens when cats and dogs are left to their own devices, the idea that cats and dogs will fight isn't made up. For that reason, you should supervise interactions between your cat and dog. Let them get acquainted with each other while you're standing by. That way, should antagonistic behavior start looming, you can put a stop to it before anyone attacks and gets hurt.

9. True. There are some exceptions that will arise due to animals' different personalities and temperaments; however, cats and dogs have been known to become great friends. But be warned: There are certain breeds of dogs that are very aggressive and prey-oriented, who will never quite take to being friends with a cat—not when they're so much fun to hunt and chase. If you have a prey-oriented dog, never permit him to be around your cat unsupervised. Keep your cat's bowls away from your dog's bowls so your dog doesn't eat your cat's food—or slobber in her water.

10. False. For the most part, no. We can't say that your cat hasn't at least thought about making these family members a meal or snack, but many times your cat's interest in them has to do with fascination with another species and curiosity about their behavior. To be on the safe side, put your small, temptingly "tasty" pets in cages or tanks that lock. If they are ever out of these enclosures, be sure to supervise them at all times while they are out. Again, while your cat probably is not looking to eat Snowball the guinea pig, why take the chance?

Give yourself a point for every correct answer. SCORE:_____

Now turn to page 217 to record your score, then head to the next quiz.

12

Cat Characteristics II

I've never understood why women love cats. Cats are inde-
pendent, they don't listen, they don't come when you call,
they like to stay out all night, and when they're home they
like to be left alone and sleep. In other words, every quality
that women hate in men, they love in a cat.

—Jay Leno

A few quizzes back, you were asked some questions about some of the characteristics that make your cat not only adorable, but also as expertly and efficiently designed as most any being in nature. Now it's time to take the second part of that quiz.

In this chapter, you'll answer more sophisticated questions—ones that not only have to do with your cat's outer appearance, but even some that will challenge you to understand specialized things about felines, including some pretty technical stuff, like genetics.

Are you up to the challenge? Do you think you know your cat inside and out? Take the following quiz and you'll soon find out.

CAT FACT

You can stop your cat from eating too fast and throwing up everything he eats. Place large, washed stones in his dish—and make sure they are too large for him to eat. Navigating around them to find his yummy kibble will actually slow him down.

QUIZ #12

Answer the following statements True or False to see how much more you know about your cat's physical traits.

1. Many white cats with blue eyes are blind.

2. The eye color kittens are born with is the eye color they will keep throughout their lives.

3. Most cats have five toes each on their front and back paws.

4. Most cats have no eyelashes—but their eyebrows perform the job of eyelashes to a point.

5. Cats have one layer of fur.

6. Your cat steps so lightly because she walks on her toes.

7. When your cat is angry about something, her pupils will show her rage by becoming large and round.

8. The incidence of the calico pattern is about even between male and female cats.

9. Because of all that fur they have, cats don't get sunburned.

10. Cats can't taste sweets.

Answers to Quiz #12

1. False. Blindness is not a trait associated with blue-eyed cats, but deafness is. That doesn't mean that all blue-eyed cats will be deaf; however, there's a 20 to 40 percent chance that a blue-eyed cat with white fur will be deaf. Interestingly enough, if a white cat has one

blue eye and one eye of a different color, the ear on the side of the blue eye will be deaf, while the cat will be able to hear from the ear on the other side.

2. False. Here's yet another way that your feline friend is closer to human beings than many other mammal groups: Cats are born with blue eyes, just like infants. Upon opening their eyes at about nine days, their eyes are blue but can change to green, brown, or even gold as she gets older.

3. False. Actually, most cats have five toes each on their front paws, but only four toes each on their back paws—eighteen digits total. However, it is not uncommon for some cats to have six—and even seven—toes each on their front paws and five toes each on their back paws. This condition is called polydactyly. Many believe cats with polydactyly exist only in North America, but their existence has been documented throughout the world.

4. True. It's truly rare to find a cat with eyelashes. Cats have whiskers that sprout above their eyes that are also known to be their eyebrows. While it's true that the eyebrows take the place of eyelashes by keeping some debris from getting into the cat's eye, this job is essentially tackled by the cat's inner eyelid.

5. False. Most cats have three coats of fur altogether. There's an outer coat, composed of "guard hairs," and two undercoats, known as "true fur," with a layer of bristly fur called "awn hairs" and a layer of soft fur called "down hairs."

6. True. No matter the breed, no cat walks on her full "foot." They all prance about on their toes. This is more obvious to see on the back paws than the front.

7. False. You don't ever want to get this mixed up! An angry cat does not have wide round pupils; rather, they are narrow, almost like lines. It's when she's excited or frightened that they grow wide and round.

8. False. The calico pattern, which means white with patches of orange, black, and red on a white cat, occurs almost always in female cats and nearly never in males. Some statistics site the ratio as being as high as 3,000 to 1. When the calico does occur in a male cat, it is caused by a genetic mutation. In addition to being very rare, male calico cats are also sterile.

9. False. Sunburn in cats is more common than most people think, and is a huge factor in cats developing skin cancer. Cats with light and white-colored fur are more susceptible to sunburn than darker-colored cats, but all should be protected if they are going to be in the sun. Sunscreens specially formulated for cats have been developed in recent years. Ask your vet to recommend one that's right for your cat.

10. True. And this can be a very good thing in that cats should not have a taste for them. Many sweets, especially chocolate, are very toxic for cats; if ingested, they can make your cat extremely sick and could even be lethal. For this reason, stick to treats made specifically for cats when you want to reward yours!

Give yourself a point for every correct answer. SCORE:_____

Now turn to page 217 to record your score, then head to the next quiz.

13

Feeding Your Cat

Cats are connoisseurs of comfort.
—James Herriot

Above all else—and this means even her naps—your cat enjoys her meals. If you've ever watched a nature documentary about big wild cats, you know that hunting down and enjoying their food is their raison d'être. In fact, lions are so passionate about their food, they will even hunt and kill—but not eat—other predatory carnivores who might stand in the way of their next meal.

This is where your cat comes from, and, as such, she maintains many of the same killer instincts. Of course, she's not going to go around hunting and slaying other cats in your house for food. Still, you can see the jungle beast in your cat. Watch her eat sometime. Does she move her head around a lot, going back and forth, then up and down, then back and forth again? There doesn't seem to be any reason for this—unless you think of how she'd have to eat her meals if she caught them herself. In order to rip the flesh from the bone, she would have to make these exact motions. It's amazing really—considering her "kill" typically comes from a bag or can.

There are so many options out there when it comes to feeding your cat, choosing her meals is enough to make your head spin. But most cat experts agree that dry food is the best alternative for feeding your cat. Moist food can be expensive and doesn't keep as long if left out in your cat's dish, but these are secondary to the health benefits of dry food. In addition to having a longer shelf life and being less expensive than moist, dry food is also excellent for your cat's dental health. If your male cat eats dry food exclusively, it is important he drinks lots of water to prevent possible lower urinary tract problems.

Appetite is one of the best ways to gauge your cat's health. Pay attention if your cat's eating habits drastically change. If she acts like she's famished no matter how much you've fed her or if she seems to have completely lost interest in eating, see your veterinarian as soon as possible; these are symptomatic of larger problems, which we'll investigate more later in the book.

So what do you really know about feeding your cat? Take the quiz to find out.

CAT FACT

Many cats don't like the taste of tap water, but all cats love fresh water, so be sure to rinse out your cat's water bowl every day. Also, cats are particularly attracted to running water, so consider purchasing a cat water fountain, available in most pet stores.

QUIZ #13

Answer the following statements True or False to get the lowdown on how your kitty chows down.

1. You should feed your cat a high-quality food, one that's high in nutrition and low in fillers.

2. Chicken bones make wonderful treats for your cat.

3. Raw liver is a safe and nutritious treat for your cat.

4. It's a good idea to feed a cat who won't eat his own food a steady diet of canned tuna.

5. Sushi isn't healthy for your cat.

6. For a really healthy kitten, substitute some of her feedings with jarred baby food.

7. A saucer of milk makes a great treat for a well-behaved kitty.

8. The best way to change your cat's brand of food is to do it all at once.

9. Cats should not be fed vegetarian diets.

10. If you run out of cat food for a few days, it's okay to go ahead and feed your cat your dog's food. If she likes it, that means she can start eating dog food exclusively.

Answers to Quiz #13

1. True. Always feed your cat the highest-quality cat food that you can afford. Many low-end foods are made up primarily of ash and other fillers, and they lack the necessary nutrients to keep your cat healthy and strong. You can start deciding what might be the best brand of food for your cat by comparing labels of foods at your local pet store. Also, why not ask your vet? And speaking of, if you are interested in supplementing your cat's diet with extra vitamins, be sure to do so only when directed by your veterinarian. There is such a thing as "too much of a good thing" when it comes to vitamins; some, if taken in too-high doses, could actually be toxic.

2. False. Yes, it's true that they love to chew on chicken bones, sucking off all the meat and good stuff on the outside, but they won't stop there. Chicken bones splinter easily and your cat depends on this: She also loves the marrow in the center. While there's nothing harmful about the marrow itself, if she swallows the bone shards, serious gastrointestinal problems could result. Your best bet, therefore, is to avoid serving these to your cat altogether.

3. False. While it might be a tempting treat for her, raw liver, fed daily in large quantities, can cause vitamin A toxicity in your cat, which can lead to many serious problems. If she likes the taste of liver, try turning her on to liver-flavored cat food or even an occasional liver-flavored cat treat instead.

4. False. Contrary to popular belief, tuna is not a great alternative to feeding your cat his regular food. In fact, too much tuna can be dangerous to a cat's health, no matter how much she loves it. There's a simple rule to follow when deciding what your cat should or should not eat: *you* are the boss. Remember, unless you give it to her, your cat won't know what tuna even tastes like, let alone decide that she's going to beg for it all the time. Keep your cat interested in her own food, which will fill all her nutritional requirements—without any hazards.

5. True. Big cats in the wild might eat salmon or other fish right out of the river: That doesn't mean raw fish is necessarily good for your "tons of years evolved into domestication" feline. Some types of raw fish can even cause a deficiency of the vitamin thiamine in cats. Again, keep your cat on a diet of her own specially formulated food and the chances will be much less that you'll run into any of these problems.

6. False. Whether you're dealing with a new kitten or a finicky geriatric cat, baby food, especially fed often, is not the best feeding alternative for your cat. Some baby foods can even be dangerous for your cat because they contain levels of onion powder for flavoring that can be extremely toxic to cats. If your cat won't eat his dry food, first try to substitute a wet food, which won't contain onion powder. And, of course, if your cat's appetite is not what it usually is, bring her to the vet to make sure another problem is not lurking.

7. False. Most people don't realize this, but cats are typically lactose-intolerant—especially when it comes to cows' milk. So serving Fluffy a saucer of milk is not necessarily giving her a treat so much as it is giving her a nasty case of stomach cramps and diarrhœa. For a happy, healthy cat, stick with water, please!

8. False. If you change your cat's brand or type of food all at once, she may not want to eat the foreign substance. Instead, you should make the change gradually over a seven- to ten-day period. This not only will help your cat get adjusted to the new flavor, but it also will prevent digestive upset that might be caused by switching foods.

9. True. Your cat is a natural carnivore and thrives on the nutrients that only a meat-based diet can provide. Your cat is not interested in tofu or carrots; don't try to get him interested in these as they really have few nutritional benefits for him. You may as well be feeding him sawdust or newspaper. Your cat has no politics when it comes to vegetarianism; if you do, of course that's totally cool. Your nutritional requirements are decidedly more vast: you are an omnivore. Your cat is not. So please don't impose a vegetarian diet on your cat.

10. False. You should not feed dog food to your cat. Just as your cat has different nutritional requirements than you, so do your cat's nutritional needs differ from your dog's. Most significantly, cats require more protein than dogs, as well as taurine, an essential amino acid not found in dog food. A taurine deficiency in cats can cause blindness and even heart failure. So while it might mean less trips to the store for you, not to mention less expense and more available storage to just buy one food for your cat and dog, you're going to have to buck up and make sure they each get their own.

Give yourself a point for every correct answer. SCORE:_____

Now turn to page 217 to record your score, then head to the next quiz.

14

Grooming Your Cat

*The man who carries a cat by the tail learns something
that can be learned in no other way.*
—Mark Twain

Cats are obsessive about their appearance, and as a result, they groom themselves often. But what many people don't realize is that what a cat does to groom herself is not always enough, and there are ways a person can—and should—help his cat groom herself, and that there are plenty more rewards for it than just a beautiful coat. A big bonus of you stepping in on the act is that it gives you an opportunity to check for fleas and ticks as well as any scratches, bumps, or suspicious lumps. But there are more satisfying reasons.

Cats don't only groom for cleanliness—especially when it comes to grooming each other; relaxation and stress relief are a big part of the ritual. And when you get in on the act, you get to share this special perk with her as well. Get her used to your grooming her when you first bring her to live with you, whether she's a kitten or a full-grown cat.

Of course, if your cat isn't taking to it as well as you had wished, it might not be relaxing for either of you. If your cat is resisting, it might be you aren't being as gentle as you thought. Try and remember how you wished your mom would brush your hair when you were a kid and go from there.

The tools you'll need to groom your cat are basic: A brush and comb will often do. Better yet, instead of using a brush, investigate using a grooming glove. The texture will feel more like a cat's tongue for your fur ball. If you have a long haired cat, you might also need to have a buzz razor handy. Long-haired cats can develop painful hair mats, which can become more painful for them when you try to brush them out. The worst ones will have to be cut. Avoid using scissors to cut out mats, because your cat will be very squirmy at the prospect of having mats removed and you may accidentally cut his skin.

And we didn't forget: The grooming process typically also includes trimming claws and oral hygiene, but we'll look at those separately later.

So you think you know all you need to know about grooming your cat? Take the next quiz to see.

CAT FACT

The best time to groom your cat is when she's relaxed, like just after she wakes up from a nap.

QUIZ #14

Answer the following statements True or False to test what you know about grooming your cat.

1. Your cat considers being groomed by you an unspeakable torture.

2. Your cat will immediately begin bathing herself after you've pet her because she thinks you're not clean enough to touch her.

3. Long-haired cats are more prone to getting hairballs than their short-haired counterparts.

4. Short-haired cats never need to be brushed.

5. Most cats spend at least 25 to 50 percent of their waking hours cleaning themselves.

6. A long-haired cat needs to be brushed every day.

7. Your cat will groom you if she feels you're not clean enough.

8. The best person to give your cat a bath is you.

9. The best way to clean your cat's ears is to submerge her head in a basin of warm water and scrub away.

10. Cats can get bad dandruff.

Answers to Quiz #14

1. False. Unless you are brushing her too roughly, your cat actually considers being groomed by you a pleasurable bonding experience.

2. False. Your cat is really not that concerned about your personal hygiene; unless you are a particularly dirty person, the amount of baths you take is entirely your business. So it's fairly safe to assume that when your cat grooms herself just after you pet her, it doesn't mean she thinks you're dirty. What she's really doing is processing one of her favorite scents: yours.

3. True. Long-haired cats are more prone to getting hairballs than their short-haired friends for a very obvious reason: They have more hair. The best way to ensure that your cat is not plagued by constant hairballs is to brush him often.

4. False. You would think that with their short coats and efficient self-bathing regimens that short-haired cats don't need you to help them maintain their coats at all, but there are reasons why brushing your short-haired cat is a good idea. For one, especially when she's in shed, the more loose hairs she has, the more she will swallow, resulting in more trouble with hairballs. Also, it's nice to develop that deep bond you get with your cat only through grooming. So how often should you brush the coat of your short-haired cat? About once a week should do the trick.

5. True. What better word is there to describe a feline than "fastidious"? And as particular as they are about their bowls being clean and their litter being scooped, they are 100 percent more obsessed with their own personal hygiene; the 25 to 50 percent approximation is conservative at best. Try to keep aware of how often your cat typically grooms herself, however, because over-grooming might indicate that she's suffering from allergies or an infestation of fleas. We'll talk more about these conditions in Chapter 34, but if your cat is cleaning herself more frequently and aggressively than usual, take her to the vet.

6. True. Perhaps this seems excessive, but the secret to keeping your long-haired cat's coat as healthy and manageable as possible is as much maintenance as possible. And the more often you brush your long-haired cat's coat, the less time you'll have to spend doing it. The recommended time to spend is fifteen to thirty minutes per day, but if you do it every day, you can probably get through her coat in less than five minutes.

7. False. Again, your cat is not as concerned with your appearance and hygiene as she is her own and will not take it upon herself to finish the job if she doesn't think you got yourself clean enough. If she does seem to "groom" you, however, this is a purely social act. Not all cats will do this, but when your cat does take it upon herself to "clean" your arm or leg, it's an expression of love and connection.

8. False. You would think that with all the positive emotional connectedness your cat associates with grooming that bathing would be the ultimate expression of love her human could show her, but this is completely wrong. Your cat likes to clean herself: she *hates* baths. And more than she hates baths, she hates anyone who would dare

subject her to that kind of malevolent torture. Do yourself a favor: If your cat needs a bath—if she's gotten too big to properly clean herself, or if she got too curious and managed to get herself covered in something harmful or just annoying—take her to a professional groomer. Many vets provide this service for their patients, but if yours doesn't, he will probably be able to give you a good recommendation.

9. False. Unless you're looking to rid yourself of all the skin that covers your hands and arms, never even think of attempting to clean your cat's ears in this manner! Instead, dip a Q-tip in baby oil and run it around the visible parts of her ear. And just as you should never jam a Q-tip (or anything else for that matter) into your own ear canal, the same applies for your cat. Be as gentle as you can, but hold her as firmly as possible. You know that your cat is a master of slipping away from you, and you don't want her to wriggle her way to getting a Q-tip lodged in her ear! Your vet can also provide appropriate ear-cleaning solutions and give you directions on how they should be used.

10. True. Some cats have dandruff, but don't break out the Head & Shoulders for your kitty. Cat dandruff is a result of, and can be controlled by, your cat's diet. In fact, she will be especially prone to dandruff if she's on a diet food—or even a senior formula—that contains less fat than a standard adult formula food. Your vet can recommend a nutritional supplement with extra fatty acids. Add this to her diet to help her rid her coat of the pesky flakes. Other causes of dandruff may include intestinal parasites, liver disease, and certain endochrine disorders, so be sure to report the dandruff to your vet.

Give yourself a point for every correct answer. SCORE:_____

Now turn to page 217 to record your score, then head to the next quiz.

15

Litter Training and Maintenance

*Cats do not have to be shown how to have a good time, for
they are unfailingly ingenious in that respect.*

—James Mason

The ability—and desire—to use a litter box is one of the characteristics of felines that sets the species far above so many other mammal groups who will simply let loose whenever and wherever they please. It shows a level of sophistication, independence, and indeed, intelligence especially lacking in equine, bovine, canine, and other groups (and we won't even get into species outside of mammals, including certain aviary antagonists who seem to actually derive pleasure from hitting inappropriate "targets." But we digress.)

The domestic cat works on instinct when she uses her litter box. In the wild, a cat is accustomed to burying her waste to throw potential predators off her scent. Incidentally, this is why cats scratch at the sides of their litter boxes; it's part of the cover-up process.

That a cat will use a litter box makes him something of a low-maintenance pet. There are no walks in zero-degree weather to fear; no humiliation of having to pick up steaming lumps with a plastic bag in public. Of course, there is the, um, *delight* of having to scoop and change cat litter—but there are ways to make even that thankless job easier. These days, in addition to traditional litter receptacles such as open pans or covered boxes, there is such a thing as a self-cleaning litter box. It may be more expensive than the alternatives, but many cat owners swear that the convenience this ingenious device provides is well worth the added cost.

Whatever you choose, be sure your cat's box is kept clean and changed regularly. If it is, he will be very thankful; if it isn't, well, let's just say he has his own charming ways to express his displeasure.

So you think you have the whole cat litter thing nailed? Take the next quiz to see for sure.

 CAT FACT

Cat litter as we know it today was invented in 1947 by a clay salesman named Edward Lowe. Before that, people would line their cat boxes with dirt, sand, and sometimes even sawdust.

QUIZ #15

Answer the following multiple-choice questions to see if your cat is happy with your litter habits.

1. How often should you change your cat's litter?

   a. Every time she uses it
   b. Once a day
   c. Once a week
   d. Once a month

2. Which material is best suited for use as a litter box?

   a. cardboard
   b. metal
   c. plastic
   d. porcelain

3. The most popular variety of cat litter is:

    a. Standard clay litter
    b. Clumping clay litter
    c. Cedar, pine, and other natural wood litters
    d. Litter made from silica crystals

4. To train a new adult cat to use the litter box, you should:

    a. Show him where it is and walk away, giving him all the privacy he needs.
    b. Put him in the box several times a day and stand over him while he's there; if he doesn't go right away, keep putting him back in the box until he does.
    c. Let him sniff it out himself—he'll really appreciate the challenge.
    d. Track litter from the box to where he usually hangs out—he'll really appreciate the gesture of you making a trail for him.

5. Which is an effective method of masking litter odor?

    a. Specially formulated cat litter deodorant
    b. Basic baking soda
    c. Aerosol air fresheners
    d. Natural odor maskers, like orange peels

6. If your cat ingests his cat litter, you should:

    a. Call your vet immediately.
    b. Call animal poison control.
    c. Read the label to see if the litter is toxic or not—then make the proper calls.
    d. Ignore it; all cat litters are manufactured to be safe for ingestion.

7. Litter box liners are:

    a. Totally unnecessary

    b. Completely useless, as your cat ends up shredding them

    c. A luxury in which you should indulge only if you want to skip a week of cleaning your cat's box here and there

    d. Essential to keeping your cat's box clean and hygienic

8. Overall, when proper precautions are taken, cleaning the litter box:

    a. Is completely safe, and easily accomplished by all family members

    b. Is highly hazardous, and should only be done by unpopular family members

    c. Is safe for some family members and not others, so discretion should be used

    d. Should be the cat's job

9. If your cat does his business outside his litter box, it could be a sign that:

    a. The box is too dirty for him to feel comfortable using.

    b. He's angry at you and acting out.

    c. He's ill and needs medical attention.

    d. All of the above.

10. To correct a cat from going outside his litter box again, you should:

    a. Hit him with a newspaper when you find the "gift" he left for you.

    b. Spray him with a water sprayer or water gun when you find the "gift" he left you.

    c. Ignore it; the shame he'll feel at being such a barbarian will be enough to stop him from ever doing it again.

d. Make sure the litter is clean and inviting and be sure to take him to the vet to make sure there's nothing physically wrong with him that would make him act out in this way.

Answers to Quiz #15

1. C. While you should scoop your cat's litter box daily, a full changing of cat litter needs to be done weekly. When you change the litter, be sure also to change the liner and scrub the box down. That will ensure the box itself stays clean and germ-free. Now, if you're the kind of person who's changing your cat's litter every time she uses it, you may just have the most spoiled cat of all time on your hands.

2. C. Why? Because that's what litter boxes are made of. A cardboard box will leak all over the place; metal is too hard and cold; if you want your cat to have a porcelain box, perhaps you should just toilet-train her. Hey, don't laugh—it has been known to happen. The downside of plastic litter boxes is that they tend to absorb kitty urine odor and will eventually smell like urine unless they are used correctly. Always line your litter box, and give it a good scrub when you change the litter. That should keep the odor away. If not, it's time to replace the pan.

3. B. Clumping litter is the most popular type of cat litter in use today. Because it clumps when moist, number one is as easy to scoop as number two, which means that the litter does not need to be changed as often. Scoop out the soiled litter, replace it with fresh, and voilà: You have a box of clean litter. But don't flush the clumps, because they will wreak absolute havoc on your septic system. Bear in mind that clumping litters are not recommended for kittens. Pieces of litter could drift into their tiny noses and obstruct their respiratory systems. They may also get this litter on their paws, and swallow it while grooming themselves, which could lead to digestive problems. There are clumping litters, however, made up of wheat and corn that are safe for kittens. Ask your vet for a recommendation.

4. A. When dealing with an adult cat, chances are almost 100 percent certain that he's used a litter box before. Cats are smart, and usually need to be shown something only once. Lead him to the litter box, let him sniff it out, and if he's ready, he'll go; if not, he'll come back to it. The only thing you will accomplish by stuffing him back into the box again and again if he isn't ready is an irate cat—and probably a few nasty scratches on your arms and hands. As far as letting him find it for himself, he probably won't appreciate the lack of hospitality on your part. If he can't find the box quickly, he'll likely show his "appreciation" by making a deposit in a place you won't want him to. And the whole "making a trail with litter bit"—that's completely a joke. Could you really imagine trails of cat litter all over your home?

5. Either A or B is acceptable here. If you chose one of these, give yourself a point. The specially manufactured stuff is effective if you want to toss out the extra bucks, but regular baking soda in and of itself also works quite well. If you're using regular litter, sprinkle the deodorizer or baking soda into the box once you have the liner in place and before you add the litter. For clumping litters, add the litter after the liner, sprinkle the baking soda or deodorizer on top, and then mix the powder into the clay. Most aerosol deodorizers only mask odors, and your cat needs to be able to sniff out where she's supposed to go and do her business. It's likely she won't want to do it in an "apple orchard" or other such locale that these artificial scents are designed to mimic. And, goodness, your cat's litter box is not a compost heap. If you think unclean litter smells bad, what do you think those orange peels will smell like in a couple of days!

6. C. Believe it or not, some kinds of cat litter are nontoxic, while others can do much damage to your cat's digestive system. Most cats regularly ingest a small amount of litter in the grooming process, and it's not harmful to them. Making a snack of litter, however, is likely not a good thing for your cat and may indicate that something else is wrong. If you catch your cat licking up a small smattering of litter as he laps himself clean, read the label on the package and take the necessary precautions. If you catch him actually snacking from his cat box, call the vet or the Animal Poison Control Center hotline at 1-888-426-4435.

7. D. Even if she partially shreds her liner in her manic attempt to "keep predators off her scent," some lining is better than none at all for the overall cleanliness of the cat box. If you have a particularly aggressive digger, try double-lining the box, or use an industrial-strength garbage bag for the purpose. In fact, wrapping a garbage bag around the pan helps litter disposal be more easy and less messy; simply pull the bag off the box and your litter is all contained without having to pour it into another bag and risk spillage.

8. C. As long as a family member has the physical strength to change a litter box, does not suffer from dust allergies (some litters are infamous for letting off a cloud of dust when poured into the pan), and has developed sense enough to know what's food and what isn't, changing a litter box can be safe for all family members. Be sure to remind children to wash their hands when done. Who is it not safe for? Pregnant women. Cat feces may contain toxoplasmosis, a protozoan parasite which can cause birth defects in fetuses. Keep in mind, however, that cats are infected by toxoplasmosis by hunting and ingesting infected birds and rodents or by eating contaminated meat. If you feel your cat is at risk, have him tested by your vet.

9. D. As we've stated many times in this book, cats are smart and extremely fastidious; if your cat's not using his litter box, there's a problem. Be sure the box is clean. If he continues to soil outside a clean box, think about whether you may have done something to irritate him—like leave him alone for a long period of time while you went on vacation. If you can rule both of these out, call your vet to determine whether something is physically wrong with your cat.

10. D. As stated above, the best way to ensure that your cat continues to use his litter box without a glitch is to keep it clean. Disciplining a cat after the fact doesn't work; he really won't know why you're spraying him with that bottle if he did his business hours before. And as we've stated again and again, hitting your cat will not teach him anything. You will have to act, however; be assured that embarrassment is not an emotion in your proud cat's repertoire.

Give yourself a point for every correct answer. SCORE:_____

Now turn to page 217 to record your score, then head to the next quiz.

16

Common Cat-tastrophes

Way down deep, we're all motivated by the same urges.
Cats have the courage to live by them.
—Jim Davis

Earlier, we looked at how to avoid many of the most common ways cats can get into trouble—and cause trouble for you by accidentally breaking or otherwise ruining your furniture and possessions. This chapter looks at common mistakes cat owners make when it comes to the health, safety, and well-being of their feline friends. Sure, some of these may seem like common sense, but cats are known to do things at times so bizarre and so cute that even the most watchful and wary of us can be prone to forgetting that some feline behavior can actually be dangerous for our cat.

How much do you know about protecting your cat from harming himself? Take the next quiz to find out.

CAT FACT

The phrase "A cat always lands on his feet" didn't fall out of the sky—no pun intended. When a cat falls, he really does fall feet first to absorb the impact.

85

QUIZ #16

Answer the following multiple-choice questions to see if you know how to keep your cat out of danger.

1. The other day, you opened one of your lower kitchen cabinets and found your cat hanging out inside.

   a. You laughed heartily and decided to let her remain until she found her own way out.
   b. You checked to make sure there was nothing unsafe or toxic in the cabinet and left the door ajar so she could come out when she was ready.
   c. You screamed at her and swatted her out of the cabinet and then you slammed the cabinet door.
   d. Your cat can't get into the cabinets; they all have child-proof safety guards on them.

2. Your cat seems to like the taste of the water in the toilet bowl more than his water dish. You:

   a. keep the lid up. It's much easier than remembering to change your cat's water every day!
   b. keep the lid up, but watch your cat carefully at all times. If she goes by the toilet, make a loud noise to startle her. She'll soon learn to stay away.
   c. try to keep the lid down, period. Train yourself to remember as it's in the best interest of your little friend.
   d. keep one toilet in your home free of human use. This way your cat can have a water source that won't cause you any worry.

3. Your cat loves to watch nature, and can often be seen pouncing at the screen of your third-floor window. You:

    a. enjoy your cat's antics, as if she's never going to actually get at her prey.

    b. make sure the screen is tightly secured. Even better—you keep her observation window either totally shut or only slightly ajar so she can't slink through.

    c. secure a harness around her so that if she falls, she doesn't fall far.

    d. forbid your cat from sitting at the window. There are many other distractions available to her besides the natural ones outside.

4. Your cat hates his carrier and seems to prefer being free to roam the car during before-and-after trips to the vet. You:

    a. let him roam. It's not like he can get into any trouble within the confines of the car.

    b. let him out a few minutes at a time and then put him back in. Do this as many times as the distance of your trip allows.

    c. put him in his carrier the night before you take him on a car trip so he can get all his complaining out of the way before you head out.

    d. keep him in his carrier at all costs. While he may complain the whole trip, he'll do so in complete safety.

5. Your cat loves playing with plastic grocery bags. You:

    a. dump out the groceries as fast as you can and litter the kitchen floor with them. It's playtime!

    b. indulge him only while under your careful supervision.

    c. tease him by playing with them yourself and then tucking them away where he can't get to them.

    d. keep your cat away from all bags—paper, canvas, plastic, or otherwise. It's a stupid way for him to keep himself occupied anyway.

6. When you bring appliances or other stuff that comes in big boxes home, your cat loves to use the empty boxes as forts. You:

   a. collapse boxes in the driveway and bring stuff upstairs without them. Your cat will never miss playing with toys that don't exist for her.
   b. let her play in the boxes under your supervision. Few things bring a cat more pleasure than tucking away in a cardboard box.
   c. play in the boxes with her. Make an afternoon of it!
   d. collapse the boxes in front of her, before she has a chance to inspect them. Let her know right off the bat that these are unsuitable for her to play with.

7. Every time you bring flowers home, your cat has to inspect them—and sometimes you can swear you've seen her lick them. You:

   a. think this is absolutely the cutest thing and let her explore away.
   b. don't bring flowers into your home unless you know they are safe as you can't always be watching your cat.
   c. never bring flowers into your home—who needs to take that risk?
   d. let your cat sniff and lick whatever comes into your house so you can see for yourself what she is and isn't allergic to.

8. Your cat loves to instigate play fights with your dog, Lily, the eighty-five-pound German shepherd. You:

   a. don't interfere. It's important for your cat to exert her dominance whenever she can.
   b. let them interact, but only under your close supervision.
   c. give Lily away. It doesn't matter who lived with you first. Your cat is your main concern and clearly this dog business is not working out.

d. always distract your cat with something else when she baits the dog.

9. Your cat's favorite hangout these days looks like your laundry hamper. You:

   a. let him hang out as long as he wants. As long as you know he's in the hamper, there's really no harm in him being there.
   b. encourage him to hang out there as long as he likes by bringing him food and water.
   c. install safety locks on your hamper so your cat can't get in.
   d. install safety locks on your hamper so your cat can't get *out*. He'll get freaked out being there and will likely never return.

10. Several times this week, your cat's played Houdini and has managed to escape the house and greet you in the driveway when you come home from work. You:

   a. let him stay outside, even after you go in. Hey, he earned the privilege!
   b. make him stay outside, even when he begs to come in. Hey, he wanted it enough and this should teach him not to be so quick to break out again.
   c. usher him inside and then make it business as usual between you and him. Try and find his exit port and be sure to seal it up as firmly as possible.
   d. turn the garden hose on him and give him a nice wet dose of discipline!

Answers to Quiz #16

1. D. Ideally, your kitchen and bathroom cabinets are already set up with childproof safety locks so your cat can't get in and explore them. If they aren't, and your cat has already learned how to paw

the door open and get in, the time to install these is now. True, there
are few things as cute as catching your cat in an unusual place, but
there's nothing at all cute about a cat accidentally swallowing a
cleaning solution. Be careful!

2. C. Make it a point to keep all toilet lids down. If you have to,
while you're getting in the habit, tape a picture of your cat to the un-
derside of the toilet lid as a reminder to keep the lid down. No one's
perfect, however. If you have a tendency to forget to put the lid
down, don't use any of those flush-cleansers, because toilet water
flavored with one of these highly toxic chemicals can cause your cat
considerable harm if swallowed.

3. B. Your best bet is to allow her to enjoy nature, while keeping
her as safe as possible while she does. Strapping a harness to her
may actually cause strangulation if she does get out. Although it's
unlikely that a cat that falls less than three stories will hurt herself,
cats that fall from three to nine stories have *more* of a chance of getting hurt than a cat that falls from more than nine stories. Why? She
won't have time to right herself and land on her feet if she falls from
less than nine stories.

4. D. While his incessant meows may annoy you the whole trip and
may make you feel sorry for him, the safest place for your cat is in
his carrier. Getting him used to it the night before, however, is a bit
cruel and selfish. And anyone who's had the experience of letting
their cat out of the carrier in the car knows that it's not the easiest
thing to get him back in—and that goes especially if you're driving!

5. B. If this is a hobby of which your cat is especially fond, let him
play with the bags for a few minutes—but don't take your eyes off
him. There are precautions you should take, however. Be sure to cut
the handles off so he can't get his neck trapped, causing strangulation. To avoid asphyxiation, slice several holes in the bag. After a

couple of minutes of inspection and frolic, he should be suitably bored to move on to the next diversion.

6. B. There's no harm in letting your cat play in the boxes as long as you're keeping an eye on her, though it is not recommended that you get in on the fun. You likely weigh considerably more than your cat, and that in and of itself could be cause for catastrophe if your weight inadvertently collapses a box she's playing in. Sure, you can collapse boxes in your driveway, but you'll only be inconveniencing yourself—and if you do it in front of her, she probably won't get the message that you don't want her to play in them. It's more likely she'll get her day's amusement watching you work.

7. B. Unfortunately for nature lovers, many household plants and flowers are dangerous to cats—and these seem to be the ones that are most appealing to them. Your best bet for keeping your cat safe and not depriving your decor of natural elements of beauty is to investigate plant and flower types before bringing them into your home—and stick with the safe ones. For more information on potentially hazardous substances to your cat, see page 108.

8. D. As tough as your cat may think she is, it's unlikely she's ever going to come out on top of a dominance match with a German shepherd. Sure, it's fine—even encouraged—for your cat and dog to be friends, but even the play fight thing can easily and unintentionally escalate to a pretty perilous situation for puss-puss. To be safe, monitor their interactions—and never leave them alone together. If your cat looks like she's going to take the dog on, immediately create a diversion for her. Chances are, your dog won't hurt your cat, but do you really want to take that chance?

9. A. It's true that there's no real harm in your silly cat hanging out in your laundry hamper—provided he's well-trained and won't soil your clothes while he's there! Most hampers are ventilated, so he won't suffocate. Save the safety locks for real dangers. Your cat is very attracted to your scent, and nowhere is it stronger than emanating from your dirty clothes. He actually derives comfort from being there. But be cautious when it comes time to actually clean those clothes. Never pour clothing directly from the hamper to the washing machine—just in case he's hiding in those dirty clothes. A washing machine is no place for a cat—on or off. Always keep the lids to both washer and dryer securely shut. If your cat has figured out how to paw these open, here's a good place for those safety locks!

10. C. There is no learnable lesson from this. By letting himself out, your cat won't feel like he's done anything wrong, and actions you take to prove him otherwise could backfire—like if you don't let him back in, he might try and find somewhere else to live. Instead, act normal and look carefully for that egress point. Remember that he's capable of slipping out of spaces that would be unimaginable for a person to get through, so be sure to cover all ground.

Give yourself a point for every correct answer. SCORE:_____

Now turn to page 217 to record your score, then head to the next quiz.

17

Cats of Famous People

*Cats are smarter than dogs. You can't get eight cats to
pull a sled through snow.*
—Television producer Jeff Valdez

Throughout the ages, many a clever cat has managed to land himself a life of celebrity, wealth, and privilege by selecting just the right human being to call his own. Some cats landed their famous humans at the height of the human's fame and fortune; many others were there for their people as they were rising to the top. And still others stood by their human's side, even if celebrity would elude them until long after their deaths.

Presidents and dignitaries, movie stars and philanthropists, authors and other notables—many famous people have been inspired, energized, and even propelled to greatness with the support of the cats they loved.

Curious about celebrity cats? Turn the page to see if you know which cats selected which famous humans.

CAT FACT

When he was the president of the United States, Ronald Reagan signed a bill that outlawed the kicking of cats.

QUIZ #17

Match up the following cats with their famous owners.

1. Socks	**a.** Winston Churchill
2. Catarina	**b.** Theodore Roosevelt
3. Muezza	**c.** The Clintons
4. Marcus	**d.** Sir Walter Scott
5. Jock	**e.** Mohammed the Prophet
6. Tabby	**f.** James Dean
7. Mysouff	**g.** Florence Nightingale
8. Misty Malarky Ying Yang	**h.** Edgar Allan Poe
9. White Heather	**i.** Queen Victoria
10. Bismarck	**j.** Amy Carter
11. Hinse	**k.** Alexander Dumas
12. Slippers	**l.** Abraham Lincoln

Answers to Quiz #17

1. C. The The Clintons' cat Socks was one of the most famous presidential cats of all time. Several books were written about him and he received tons of fan mail while in the White House. Actually belonging to First Daughter Chelsea, Socks was found as a kitten, abandoned under Chelsea's piano teacher's porch. When the Clintons left the White House, they gave Socks to the president's secretary, Betty Currie, as he and the Clintons' chocolate Lab, Buddy, did not get along.

2. H. An impoverished Edgar Allan poe appointed his tortoiseshell cat, Catarina (sometimes spelled "Cattarina") his dying wife's official nurse (more like a heating pad). Virginia was dying of consumption in the winter of 1846, and Poe could not afford to heat his home. So impressed was Poe with Catarina's devotion and loyalty to her sick mama that he wrote "The Black Cat" in her honor.

3. E. Mohammed the Prophet had a cat named Muezza, whom he simply adored. Rumor has it that once when he went to pray, the cat was peacefully sleeping on the sleeve of his robe. Rather than disturb his dozing friend, he cut off the sleeve of his robe and let the feline continue her nap.

4. F. James Dean's kitten, Marcus, was a gift to him from Elizabeth Taylor. The night before Dean's fatal car crash, he gave Marcus to his friend, Jeanette Mills, with instructions on feeding Marcus and a note for his vet.

5. A. Winston Churchill didn't know ginger-colored Jock for very long, but he was still quite devoted to his kitten. When Churchill was dying, Jock stayed in his bed with him. Churchill was so glad for the tiny fur ball's attention, he even named Jock in his will.

6. L. Abraham Lincoln was a huge cat lover, and Tabby was the name of four presidential cats while Lincoln and his family lived at the White House.

7. K. Alexander Dumas, author of *The Three Musketeers*, had a cat named Mysouff. It was said that Mysouff had extrasensory powers, especially when it came to what time Dumas would finish his work.

8. J. Misty Malarky Ying Yang was the name of First Daughter Amy Carter's Siamese cat, who was especially fond of steak and seafood from the White House kitchen.

9. I. White Heather was the name of the much-beloved black-and-white Persian Queen Victoria kept in her later years. Upon her death, the cat was entrusted to her son, the new king, Edward VII.

10. G. Bismarck was the name of a large Persian cat whom Florence Nightingale had adored, but it is said that the famous nurse shared her home with more than sixty cats in her lifetime.

11. D. Sir Walter Scott's giant tomcat, Hinse, had a reputation for terrorizing dogs—especially Scott's own bloodhound, Nimrod. Unfortunately for Hinse, in 1826 Nimrod lost patience with the feisty feline and killed him.

12. B. Slippers, a grayish mixed-breed tabby with extra toes on each foot, was the beloved cat of President Theodore Roosevelt.

Give yourself a point for every correct answer. SCORE:_____

Now turn to page 217 to record your score, then head to the next quiz.

18

Kitty Playtime

When I play with my cat, how do I know that she is not
passing time with me rather than I with her?
—Montaigne

I s there any animal more playful than the domesticated cat?
The answer is easy: not even close. Cats adore their playtime
and typically try to get as much of it in as possible. And for good
reason.

Playtime is essential to your cat—but it's not because she's an in-
satiable hedonist. Your cat uses her playtime the same way you use
your time at the gym—for exercise. A cat that doesn't get enough
playtime runs several health risks, including obesity.

It's easy—and let's face it, lots of fun—to make sure your cat gets
enough exercise. It's rare that a cat won't show some interest in a
string bouncing on a stick or a rolling ball. To watch him stalk and
pounce and bat with his precious paw is a source of great joy for any
cat lover.

So what do you know about your cat's exercise requirements?
Take the following quiz to find out.

 CAT FACT

Your cat may adore catnip, but keep in mind that a little goes a long way.
Half a teaspoon will usually do the trick!

QUIZ #18

Answer the following statements True or False to test what you know about cats and playtime.

1. To give your cat a great workout, chase her around your house or apartment.

2. Playing with string with your cat is a bad idea because your cat could ingest the twine.

3. Being good at playtime is essential for a kitten's overall development.

4. Your cat considers playtime with you a bonding experience.

5. Small objects make excellent cat toys.

6. It's a good idea to play with your cat around the same time every day.

7. Want your cat to sleep through the night? Make his exercise time come right before your bedtime.

8. There is such a thing as too much exercise for your cat.

9. Older cats lose interest in exercise and should not be encouraged to play.

10. It's okay to play aggressively with your cat; she understands it's just play.

Answers to Quiz #18

1. False. While it can be hilarious to play "hunter" and "hunted" with your cat, you have to be careful about how enthusiastic a pred-

ator you come off as being. Chasing your cat around your house or apartment, if she's taking your hunt seriously, could actually be perceived as a real threat!

2. True and False (give yourself a point either way). There are lots of ways to make sure your cat gets the exercise he needs, but as with any method of play, you must keep it safe. As we discussed in chapter 8, loose ribbons, rubber bands, and even string can be extremely dangerous to your cat—if she decides to eat them. But you can make it so that can't be possible by securely attaching any of these to a stick—and any cat owner knows that the string game is always a hands-down (paws-up) winner!

3. True. As is the case with human babies, playtime for kittens is about much more than pure entertainment. Kittens develop all kinds of skills when they learn to play together. Coordination and pouncing, stalking and running, climbing and "hunting" all prepare a kitten to deal with its environment as well as stimulate intellectual, behavioral, and physiological growth. In addition, playtime encourages kittens to be self-sufficient (Mama is not going to wrestle littermates for me) and also teaches "social skills" (there's a difference between play biting and actual biting).

4. True. Despite how cute your cat looks when he's in on the act of playing, one of the biggest bonuses of kitty playtime is that it's something you and your cat can share, giving you yet another special way to bond. When moms and dads get in on the fun, playtime takes on a whole new level for cats.

5. False. It may seem weird, but one of the most helpful ways to decide what is or isn't safe for your cat is to think of your cat as being a toddler—with the same curiosity, judgment ability, and tendency to put foreign objects in her mouth and even swallow them. Never give your cat an object smaller than her own mouth to play with. If she swallows it, the best-case scenario is that it will pass through her digestive system and end up in her litter box; on the other side of the spectrum, she could either choke on the object or it can become lodged in her digestive tract. There are plenty of toys available that make playtime safe, not dangerous.

6. True. As we've said earlier, cats are creatures who crave routine; therefore, the more routines you incorporate into your cat's life, the happier he will be. Perhaps you can establish playtime for the minutes before going to work, while having your coffee and reading the paper. If you rush around too much in the morning to even consider adding another activity to your own hectic routine, perhaps playtime can happen right after you get home from work? Your cat will enjoy the added bonus of having special bonding time with you along with the wonderful gift of your being back home with him.

7. True. If you've ever played for a long time with your cat, you know that an especially active play session will tucker him right out, and you can be sure a nice long nap will follow. Some people worry that too much playtime will have the opposite effect—that their cats will be so overstimulated from so much play that they'll be up all night bouncing off the walls. Don't forget that there are few things a cat loves more than sleep, and the chances are greater that she is more likely to take advantage of the opportunity to catch some z's than not.

8. True. Cats play the way they sleep; frequently, but in short bursts at a time. When you play with your cat, limit the activities to about fifteen minutes at a time. This way, your cat won't overexert himself.

9. False. While your older cat may not have all the zeal your kitten has over batting Ping-Pong balls about in the bathtub, that doesn't mean she's done with play for good; she just can't play as much as she did when she was young. As a cat gets older, it becomes easier and easier for her to put on weight. She needs to be encouraged to have an outlet to work off her meals, and it's your job to get her interested in mild physical activity.

10. False. It can be lots of fun instigating your cat to aggressive behavior, but there may be ramifications to it. For example, your cat might not realize that you are just kidding. Especially if you are a person of considerable height and girth, you could really terrify her by being too aggressive. Another reason to keep play between you and your cat fairly tame is so she won't believe it's okay to play rough with every human she encounters. Though her swatting and nipping at your own hand might be amusing to you, it could cause a whole lot of trouble for everyone if she bites a visitor—especially a child.

Give yourself a point for every correct answer. SCORE:_____

Now turn to page 217 to record your score, then head to the next quiz.

19

Kitty Obesity

*Cats are a mysterious kind of folk. There is more passing
in their minds than we are aware of.*
—Sir Walter Scott

Afat cat is a happy cat—right? Wrong! Just as an overweight
human faces many challenges—physical, emotional, and social
among them—so does your kitty. And we hate to tell you this, but it's
really not the cat's fault if he's overweight. If you have a fat cat,
chances are you are to blame.

How can you prevent your cat from plumping up? Be careful
what you feed her. Check cat food labels for nutritional information.
Just as there's junk food for people, so there is for cats. And unless
doctor's orders call for it, never feed her more than the recommended daily allowance on the label. In fact, your best bet is to feed
her just slightly less. Cat food manufacturers will encourage cats to
eat more—that's what they're in business for after all.

In addition to monitoring your chubby kitty's diet, make sure he
gets plenty of exercise. It's more common now than ever that a cat
will spend his entire life indoors, and that means a significant decrease in exercise compared with his grandfathers and great-
grandfathers.

Are you making sure your cat keeps within a healthy weight? Take
the next quiz to find out!

OAT FACT

Giving a 10-pound cat a 20-calorie treat is like giving a 150-pound person a 300-calorie treat.

QUIZ #19

Answer the following multiple-choice questions to see what you know about cats and obesity.

1. How often should you feed your adult cat?

   a. Always keep a full bowl of dry food available to her.
   b. Every time she's hungry.
   c. Twice a day.
   d. Every other day.

2. Is it a good idea to feed your cat from the table?

   a. Never. A cat eats cat food and a human eats human food!
   b. Sometimes. When we have something for dinner Poofy really likes, we give her a special treat.
   c. Absolutely. Our cat is like a member of our family. If it's good enough for us to eat, it's good enough for her.
   d. We don't feed our cat from the table, but sometimes she manages to steal from us.

3. Do cats naturally know when to stop eating?

   a. Of course they do. They're smart enough to know when they're full.
   b. A cat will eat until it's just under full. They are very conscious of maintaining a good weight.
   c. A cat will eat until it's full, but will go back again for seconds if she really likes the food being offered and if there's any left in the bowl.
   d. A cat will only stop eating if there's no more food in the bowl.

4. A cat should be rewarded with treats:

   a. Always.
   b. Sometimes.
   c. Never.
   d. You mean they make treats for cats?

5. Which of these is *not* a good way to exercise your cat?

   a. Buy a harness and a leash and walk her around the neighborhood.
   b. Put her on your treadmill.
   c. Play with her often and leave toys out for her when you aren't home.
   d. Get her a kitten.

6. How much should a standard house cat weigh?

   a. About 5 pounds
   b. About 7 pounds
   c. About 10 pounds
   d. About 16 pounds

7. How much weight will a pregnant cat typically gain?

   a. About 5 percent of her normal body weight
   b. About 15 percent of her normal body weight
   c. About 25 percent of her normal body weight
   d. About 35 percent of her normal body weight

8. Which of the following diseases can be brought on by kitty obesity?
   a. Diabetes
   b. Heart disease
   c. Liver disease
   d. All of the above

9. What is the likelihood that a cat will be overweight if his owner is also a couple of sizes too many?

    a. One has nothing to do with the other.

    b. An overweight cat *always* means its mom and dad are overweight.

    c. Sometimes a cat can be overweight even if its mom and dad are thin.

    d. It's more likely than not that an overweight cat lives in a household of hefty humans.

10. Compared with the weight gain your human frame can handle, three or four extra pounds on your cat is like carrying:

    a. three or four extra pounds

    b. ten to fifteen extra pounds

    c. twenty to thirty extra pounds

    d. fifty or more extra pounds

Answers to Quiz #19

1. C. The ideal way to feed your cat is to offer her dry food twice a day. This is not always possible, however, because people generally have lives outside of the care and maintenance of their cats (someone has to pay for that kibble, right?). If you can feed your cat only once a day, give her less than the recommended allowance of cat food. When you get back to her, you can always make up the difference. For felines, it's much easier to gain weight than to lose it.

2. A. As cruel as it seems, your cat does not need to have a place set at your dinner table. Ever. Cats and humans have very different dietary needs. As much as she begs to share your dinner, keep her interest in her own bowl. Cat food is designed with her special dietary needs in mind. And it's also made in convenient bite-size bits, which means choking will not be likely (whereas if she steals a chicken bone from your plate, she might not be so lucky). True, begging may seem slightly cute at first, but it gets old fast—so don't encourage it.

3. C. It's for this reason that you should not put a whole day's food supply in your cat's bowl at once—and especially if she really likes the taste of her food!

4. B. Treats can reinforce good behavior in cats, so once in a while, when they've done something worth the reward, it's okay to give your cat a treat. Be sure to read labels, however. Like human treats, cat treats are not always nutritionally sound. Hey, that's why they call them "treats."

5. B. No kidding here: Never put your cat on a treadmill or any exercise device in your home gym. A cat likes to be in control of the action. A treadmill may not only scare her, she could get seriously hurt on it.

6. C. A standard domestic short-haired cat, the most common pet when it comes to cats, should weigh around ten pounds. There are exceptions, of course. If your fully grown male Maine Coon weighed twelve pounds, you'd probably be able to see right through him! For more specific information on cat breeds, refer back to chapter 3.

7. C. A female's body weight will increase between 20 and 25 percent when pregnant. A healthy cat should be able to lose this weight naturally after the birth.

8. D. Remember, a chubby cat is not a happy cat—nor is she a particularly healthy cat. If you have an obese cat, take her to see the vet and get her checked out for these problems. Your vet will perform a few tests and be able to discern whether she's suffering from any of these diseases and also how to treat the condition. No doubt, your vet will also give you some good weight-loss tips for your cat!

9. D. Bad habits and behavior, unfortunately, typically beget bad habits and behavior. It's not good for you or your cat to be overweight. Do yourself a favor and admit that your pants are too tight and do something about it. By being more conscious of your diet and exercise habits, you'll be more aware of hers as well and then everyone wins!

10. D. Three or four extra pounds on you is nothing; on your cat, it translates to carrying about fifty extra pounds—and that's way too much! In addition to being horrible for her physical health, think of her mental and emotional health. When a cat is overweight, she cannot function like a cat does. She tires easily. She becomes horizontally bound (when's the last time you saw a jumbo-size kitty leap up onto a windowsill to watch the birds?). Do your cat a favor: Keep her fit and trim so she can enjoy her life to the fullest!

Give yourself a point for every correct answer. SCORE:_____

Now turn to page 217 to record your score, then head to the next quiz.

Cats are among the most curious creatures in creation. This curiosity keeps them constantly exploring and interacting with their environments, learning as much as they can about their surroundings. Unfortunately, this constant exploring and interacting with their environments sometimes puts them in peril. For this reason, it is essential to cat-proof your home and also take precautions around the yard if your cat is an indoor-outdoor kitty.

Your cat is essentially a sturdy, resilient being, but there are certain things that, if ingested, could make her very sick or even kill her. For example, the Easter lily is so toxic to a cat, it can cause severe kidney damage if she finds it irresistible enough to eat. She may also eat things that are not quite as aesthetically appealing, like your medication—or even her own when she's not supposed to be taking it. Always consult your veterinarian before giving any medication to your cat.

Below is a list of common cat toxins. Some of these may seem obvious, but others may surprise you. So where does the danger lie?

Around the house:

- acetaminophen
- aspirin
- batteries
- chocolate
- cleaning products
- coffee
- liquid potpourri
- ribbons
- table salt

In the shed or garage:

- antifreeze
- citronella candles
- fertilizers
- insecticides
- rodent bait
- swimming pool treatment supplies

Some natural toxins include:

- aloe
- avocado
- azaleas
- caladiums
- daffodils
- gladiolas
- holly
- hyacinths
- hydrangeas
- irises
- lilies
- morning glories
- oleander
- onions
- poinsettias
- rhododendrons
- sweet peas
- tulips
- yucca

There are many more substances that are toxic to your cat; please consult with your vet before introducing anything into your home to determine its toxicity.

20

How Your Cat Communicates with You

My cat does not talk as respectfully to me as I do to her.
—Colette

As any cat lover knows, communication between cats and their human is a huge proof that you don't need to speak the same language to be able to get your points across. When a cat and a person share a good bond, for the most part, they understand one another and are able to satisfy each other's particular needs.

First, there's a basic system of sounds your cat makes that can give you a pretty good idea of what she's feeling. A cat who purrs is typically happy. When she growls, she feels threatened and is warning off perceived predators. When she trills, she's usually excited about something—maybe to see you, maybe to see you holding a pack of her favorite cat treats. And then there are those non-auditory clues that speak volumes: the nose nibble, the head rub, you know the ones we mean.

But does your cat speak your language? Many cat lovers will insist that their feline friends know exactly what they're saying to them, but in reality, what your cat goes by is your tone and your actions. You can tell your cat in a soft voice while you're petting her that you think she's a dummy, and she'll still bump against you and purr. And as many nice things as you say to your cat while you're screaming at her from across the room, she won't get it. It's all a matter of interpretation: hers.

So you think you know what your cat is saying to you, do you? Take the next quiz to find out for sure.

CAT FACT

A cat does not purr when she's fast asleep, no matter how happy, content, or comfortable she is.

QUIZ #20

Answer the following statements True or False to see if you understand what your cat's been trying to tell you.

1. When your cat hides away, she's playing a game. In reality, she wants you to find her.

2. When your cat is happy, she holds her tail high and steady.

3. When your cat rubs her face against yours, it means she thinks she owns you.

4. When a cat sits at the window and makes a chattering noise, it means she's trying to make friends with the birds and squirrels and other wildlife she sees.

5. When a cat hisses, it always means she's seriously angry.

6. Cats have been known to grunt.

7. When your cat makes direct eye contact with you, it means she trusts you.

8. No matter what's going on with her, you know your cat is happy and content if she's purring.

9. When your cat blinks at you, she's telling you that she loves you.

10. When a cat grooms you, she's telling you that she thinks you need to take more thorough showers.

Answers to Quiz #20

1. False. Yes, your cat is a playful creature. And yes, she loves to play with you. But hide-and-seek is not one of the games she likes to play. When your cat hides, she wants some alone time. If you happen upon her in one of these private moments, maybe if you have to get something in your closet and she's curled up in your shoes, try as hard as you can to ignore her. If she decides quiet time is over, she'll come out and start looking for you.

2. True. Next to purring, nothing says "happy cat" like a high tail when she walks. When her tail is lowered and lashing back and forth, she's on high alert and telling you to stay back; when it's lowered, she's telling you to stay away or it's likely she'll attack. And when a cat is angry or frightened, her tail will likely bristle up.

3. True. Rubbing her face against you is a high compliment in cat expression. When a cat sees something she'd like to "own," she marks it by rubbing the side of her mouth against it. Of course, cats do like to "own" just about everything they see! But when your cat rubs his nose up against your nose, take it as the ultimate compliment. This is one of the most intimate gestures she will make, and she won't do it to just any human—just the ones, or one, she loves the most!

4. False. As cute and cuddly and lovey as your cat can be, don't forget that by nature, she is a predator and avid hunter. So when she's staring out the window, switching her tail back and forth, and

making that odd chattering sound, it means that not only is she strategizing how to pounce the prey in her sights, but also anticipating the pleasure of crushing it up in her jaw once she's made the catch.

5. False. Typically, a cat only hisses when she's seriously annoyed or angry; however, a cat at play might hiss at her feline playmate — or even at her human — merely because she's gotten really into the game and not because she intends to show any ill will at all.

6. True. As weird as it seems, the truth of the matter is that cats have lots of odd sounds they are capable of making, and a grunt is one of them. Typically, it's a lazy cat who finds meowing too much work who may grunt to greet you.

7. True. Cats are wary creatures. They are predators by nature, and, as a result, can be extremely cautious about letting their guard down: What hunts can also be hunted. For this reason, they will rarely make eye contact with any living thing that could possibly attack at any moment. But the rules are different with you. He knows you well enough to realize you mean him no harm; therefore, he will not only make direct eye contact with you but may even engage in staring contests with you now and again.

8. False. That a cat only purrs when she's happy is one of the biggest misunderstandings a human can have with a feline. A cat will also purr when she's extremely nervous or in pain. The best way to understand if your cat is purring for pure pleasure is with logic and common sense. Think of it in terms of the situation. If your cat is purring in the vet's office, she's probably not feeling jolly and is likely worried that she's going to get pinched or pricked with a needle or worse. Vets are wonderful people, it's true, but that doesn't mean your cat is ever happy to see hers. Of course, if your cat is purring because she's sitting in your lap, about to drift off for a nap, you can pretty much bet that it's because she's in a state of perfect pleasure.

9. True. Though there really is no scientifically documented study to back up this claim, it relates back to the answer in question 7. Just as a cat is wary to stare in just anyone's eyes, so is he wary to look away from another creature with whom he's holding glances. By closing and opening his eyes for you, or blinking, he's showing you that he trusts nothing will happen to him if he looks away from you. And if you blink lovingly at him, you can easily show him you feel the same way.

10. False. A cat who grooms her human is showing affection to that person, and nothing more—unless the human happens to have cat food on his hand. In that case, it's safe to say that the cat's major motivation is to savor the flavor as she licks it off.

Give yourself a point for every correct answer. SCORE:_____

Now turn to page 217 to record your score, then head to the next quiz.

21

Spaying and Neutering

*It is a very inconvenient habit of kittens that whatever you
say to them, they always purr.*
—Alice, from *Alice in Wonderland* by Lewis Carroll

O ne day, you have a playful, semi-rambunctious female kitten running around your house, causing only the mildest amount of
chaos in your life. The next day, you have a howling banshee, who's
literally climbing the walls—and windows—trying to get out. Or
maybe you have a feisty male kitten, who one day decides it's okay to
be aggressive with you and even spray his urine in your house. What's
going on?

Brace yourself: Your baby is growing up. Boy or girl, these peculiar
behaviors actually indicate that your kitten is starting to exhibit signs
of sexual maturity. If you're a cat breeder (see page 135), then this is a
very exciting time for you. Your kittens are almost ready to start having kittens of their own. If you're not, this can be a nightmare. On top
of the havoc your little one is beginning to wreak, you also have to face
facts that it's time for your cutie pie to go under the knife. Luckily,
being altered is a much more stressful experience for you than for your
little one. Within a few days, he or she will completely forget the experience. Of course, the first few days before and after the procedure will
likely be some of the most trying and guilt-ridden days of your life.

Do yourself a favor and let it go: Altering your cat is one of the best
things you can do for him or her; in this situation more than so many
others, the benefits well outweigh the negatives.

What do you know about having your kitten altered? Take the following quiz to find out.

CAT FACT

According to Yahoo! Pets Cat Tips, one female cat and one male cat and their offspring can produce 420,000 cats in seven years!

QUIZ #21

Answer the following statements True or False to see what you know about altering your cat.

1. It's healthier for your cat to have him or her fixed.

2. When a male cat is neutered, his penis is removed.

3. The best time to fix a cat is after he or she has experienced his or her first mating.

4. Neutering usually requires the male cat to stay in the cat hospital overnight.

5. When a female cat is spayed, her ovaries and uterus are removed.

6. Your cat will despise you forever if you have him or her fixed.

7. A neutered male cat will be less aggressive than a male cat who has not been neutered.

8. A cat will no longer spray once it's been fixed.

9. Both spaying and neutering are reversible.

10. A cat should be at least four months old before it is spayed or neutered.

Answers to Quiz #21

1. True. In addition to being healthier to cats as a whole by preventing overpopulation, it is healthy for your cat to be altered in an individual sense. Female cats who are spayed are no longer at risk for uterine or ovarian cancer. There is also a tremendous reduction in the incidence of breast cancer for female cats spayed prior to their first heat. Male cats are no longer susceptible to testicular cancer, but also will not fight as much, increasing their chances of survival. Also, by suppressing the urge for your cat to get out and mate, you've decreased his or her drive to break out into the world and put him- or herself in the path of possible peril.

2. False. Your male cat still needs his penis to urinate. When a cat is neutered, only his testicles are removed.

3. False. As it is with humans so it is with cats: It only takes one time for the female to get pregnant. You don't want to wait that long. Ideally, the best time to alter your cat is before he or she begins to exhibit sexually motivated behavior, at about six months old.

4. False. Nope. In this case, the guys get lucky. Neutering is an outpatient procedure because there's really no internal work done; you can usually take your male cat home right after the procedure. The experience you'll have with a female kitten, on the other hand, is decidedly more traumatic. For her, it is surgery—and abdominal surgery at that. She will not be permitted to eat or drink after midnight the night before her procedure. (Please note: nor will your male kitten be able to eat or drink past midnight the night before.) You must leave her with the vet, no matter how pitifully she meows, and you will not be able to pick her up until the following day. When she comes home, her leg and belly will be shaved, and she will need to wear a stockingette or an Elizabethan collar until her stitches heal—about ten days. She will not like either outfit and will try to free herself often to get access to her tummy so she can tear out the stitches with her teeth. If you can stay home with her for at least a couple of days after the procedure, do. She will be groggy from the anesthesia, weak as a kitten—literally—and will need you to make sure she doesn't destroy her doctor's handiwork before she heals!

5. True. Spaying entails surgery to remove both your female cat's ovaries and uterus. In recent years, advancements in the technique, have deemed the procedure less traumatic for her—and for her human. In some cases, sterilization drugs have been employed, but for the most part, vets stick to the old standard.

6. False. We can't stress this enough: Your cat will be a little confused and traumatized at first—this has mostly to do with any trip he or she has to make to the vet—but your cat will not hate you for altering him or her, at least not as much as you hate yourself for it!

7. True. This is not to say your male cat won't be aggressive at all, but because he no longer feels the need to dominate everything— and everyone—to prove he is the best possible candidate for mating, he will mellow out considerably once his procedure is performed.

8. False. While this aggravating trait will be mostly stopped by altering your cat, there are some that never lose this territorial tendency. For tips on how to get it under control, see chapter 28, "Dealing with Aggressive Behavior."

9. False. Neither of these procedures is reversible.

10. True. There are so many developmental things going on with your cat before she's four months old, or sixteen weeks, that it really is less taxing for the cat if you can wait. Usually sexual behavior

starts to be exhibited around six months, and that's generally recommended to be the best time; of course, your best bet is to consult
with your vet, who, from examining your kitten and administering
inoculations, already knows your individual kitten and will have a
pretty good sense of when it's time.

Give yourself a point for every correct answer. SCORE:_____

Now turn to page 217 to record your score, then head to the next quiz.

22

Declawing and Tendonectomy

If animals could speak the dog would be a blundering out-
spoken fellow, but the cat would have the rare grace of
never saying a word too much.
—Mark Twain

A ll cats scratch—but why? The answer is that it makes them comfortable to, and on many levels. First, cats scratch to shed worn-out claw sheathes when new ones come in. On top of that, they also scratch when they are nervous, stressed, and even bored. The problem is your cat doesn't always exercise great judgment when it comes to deciding what to scratch, which leads cat owners to take matters into their own hands—and not always in their cats' best interests.

Declawing, also known as onychectomy, is one of the most common procedures cat owners seek to protect their things from the destructive claws of their cat. Not every cat is declawed, however, and there's good reason for this: Declawing a cat involves removing the entire top of each digit in your cat's front paws; it's not a cosmetic procedure, it's an amputation. General wisdom recommends that the owner exhaust all possible options before considering this one; if all else fails, and the alternatives are to bring the cat to a shelter or have it euthanized, then claw removal becomes essential. Once a cat's claws are removed, however, he must forever remain strictly an indoor cat—not such a bad thing—as he will be unable to properly protect himself in the outside world.

A humane alternative to declawing is tendonectomy. In this procedure, instead of removing the claw, or, in reality, the tops of the paws, the tendons that allow the cat to extend and retract her claws are cut. Said to be less painful for the cat than declawing, it also entails a significantly shorter recovery time. And the cat gets to keep his paws intact and his claws, even though he can no longer use them. Tendonectomy does, however, come with its own share of negatives. Do you know what they are? If you don't, you will by the time you finish this chapter.

Before you decide on either of these options, be sure to consult with your vet and get his opinion. He may be able to recommend a training method you haven't yet tried. Hey, you never know! In addition, your vet may recommend a product called Soft Paws. These are nontoxic, soft plastic nail caps that are glued onto the claws once a month.

Now head to the quiz to see how much you really know about your cat and his claws.

CAT FACT
Cats are very proud and usually hide pain, discomfort, and illness quite well.

QUIZ #22

Answer the following statements True or False to see what you know about your cat and his claws.

1. A cat that keeps her claws will shred all your furniture and ruin your life.

2. Claws are retractable; if your cat does not want to scratch something, she doesn't have to just because she touches it.

3. Declawing a cat is a painless procedure.

4. Declawing is against the law in many countries, including England, Germany, and Switzerland.

5. When a cat is declawed, only his front claws are surgically removed.

6. Cats love having their nails done, and some will even let you file and paint their claws when you're done clipping.

7. If your cat has a tendonectomy, you will need to be vigilant about keeping his nails trimmed.

8. A tendonectomy is a painless procedure.

9. The best way to trim your cat's claws is with a standard nail clipper.

10. You *can* train your cat not to use his claws where you don't want him to.

Answers to Quiz #22

1. False. Anyone who takes this stance is being overly dramatic and hasn't done anything actively to try to stop the scratching. Do yourself a favor: Act. First, invest in a scratching post or scratching mat. When you bring it into your house, show your cat the special treat you got for her and show her it's okay for her to scratch that to her heart's content. As long as she has something to scratch, it's likely she won't go after your furniture anymore. If she does, she can be trained not to, which we'll cover later.

2. True. A cat does not have to scratch something just because she touches it; scratching is a conscious choice she makes. When she's playing with another cat, when she's batting at her toys, when she pats the face of her favorite human—these are all times she puts

those treacherous talons away. The trick, then, is to teach your cat to keep her claws to herself when it comes to your furniture, which is not an impossible feat. It just requires time and patience.

3. False. *False* is almost not even a strong enough word to describe how completely untrue this statement is. Imagine if you had an operation to remove the top portion of all of your fingers. Not only would it cause you excruciating physical pain, but deep emotional pain would also result. Maybe you pay little attention to your fingernails—or maybe you're obsessed with having them perfectly manicured at all times. Either way, you're going to miss your fingertips. A cat is emotionally invested in her claws. Not only will not having them make her feel insecure and unable to protect herself, she also uses them for agility and balance and even in her grooming rituals. Is declawing a *painful* procedure? On all levels, yes!

4. True. So cruel is the concept of essentially removing a cat's "fingertips" that many countries around the world have outlawed it altogether. Interestingly enough, the United States and Canada are *not* among the countries who consider this a barbaric and inhumane procedure.

5. False. While it's standard practice to remove only the front claws, as these are the ones that cause the most damage, sometimes back claws are also removed in this procedure.

6. False. While "cat enjoying manicure" is a comical visual, anyone who has a cat with claws, and who's in charge of clipping those claws, knows nothing could be further from the truth. A cat depends on her paws, and she does not like for them to be touched. This is the first problem. A cat, as we learned earlier, uses his claws for many things, and as such is very protective of them. Number two. And finally, number three, a cat absolutely hates being held against her will. This is one of the times that would definitely rate that way. Still, taxing as it is for you both, it has to be done. The best way is to sit on the floor with your legs outstretched. Then, pick up your cat and gently fold her into a sitting position, facing away from you. Hold her securely with one arm, between your knees. With trimmers at the ready, give her paw a little squeeze with the arm you're holding her in and her claws will come out. Carefully trim only the top "hooked" portion of her claws. This procedure might not prove to be as easy as it reads, so don't be surprised if you need to enlist a partner to help you in the task.

7. True. When your cat loses the ability to flex her claws and scratch for herself, there's no way she can wear her nails down anymore. Therefore, you have to be on top of trimming her claws — about once every week to two weeks in the spring and summer and roughly every three to four weeks in the fall and winter. Otherwise, your cat's claws will become ingrown in her foot pads, causing numerous other problems.

8. False. We can't sugarcoat things for you and tell you that your cat won't experience any pain in a tendonectomy; it's surgery after all. After the procedure, your vet will keep her for at least twenty-four to forty-eight hours and will likely administer regular pain medication to keep her comfortable. By the time she comes home, she should be feeling much better, but you must be cautious with her paws. Don't grab them. Watch as she moves around on them. If she's not stepping in her regular fashion in a week or so, call the vet to make sure she isn't experiencing complications, such as an infection.

9. False. Look at your nail beds. Now look at your cat's. Your nails are essentially flat, while hers are round. Now, certainly you *could* trim her nails with your clippers. Just know that this is not going to be the most comfortable option for her. Come on, get her her own trimmers. It's a few bucks' investment that will make a considerable difference.

10. True. As we've covered so far in several other areas of this book, your cat is actually trainable. Through consistent training, you can ensure that your cat won't scratch your furniture. Just remember the startle effect of a few carefully placed paper cup towers!

Give yourself a point for every correct answer. SCORE:_____

Now turn to page 217 to record your score, then head to the next quiz.

23

Your Cat's Oral Hygiene

The cat does not offer services. The cat offers itself. Of course he wants care and shelter. You don't buy love for nothing. Like all pure creatures, cats are practical.
—William S. Burroughs

A lot of cat lovers tend to overlook one big component of their cat's health: their teeth. As a tried-and-true carnivore, your cat's teeth are one of the most significant attributes of her physiology. Without them, it is considerably more difficult for her to eat. And it's not like they make dentures for cats—and if they did, good luck getting your cat to wear them!

Looking after your cat's oral health is not that difficult or time consuming. It's just another way you can show your feline friend that you care about her—about *all* of her.

So you think you know something about caring for your cat's teeth? Take the following quiz to see just how much you really know!

CAT FACT
Many vets' offices are now equipped with digital X-ray technology, making it much easier for them to detect dental distress.

QUIZ #23

Answer the following statements True or False to see if you truly understand the importance of your cat's oral hygiene.

1. You don't need to brush your cat's teeth. A good dry cat food will keep your cat's teeth clean.

2. You should check your cat's teeth and gums regularly for plaque buildup, oral abscesses, broken teeth, cavities, and other dental problems.

3. Cats love the taste of many of the toothpastes people use.

4. You should get your cat used to toothbrushing from the time he is a kitten.

5. One way to get your cat used to brushing is to massage his gums with your fingers.

6. Cat treats are extremely high in sugar and should be avoided at any cost.

7. Make toothbrushing a rewardable chore by brushing your cat's teeth *before* mealtime.

8. Flossing is extremely important for your feline's oral health.

9. Bad oral hygiene can cause serious medical problems in your cat.

10. If a cat has a bad tooth, nature will see to it that it simply falls out on its own.

Answers to Quiz #23

1. False. While dry food does a much better job of keeping your cat's teeth clean than wet food, it doesn't do the full job. Head to your lo-

cal pet store and pick up a toothbrush and paste for your cat. The rest of the answers in this chapter will tell you how to take it from there.

2. True. Your cat's overall health includes her oral health, so you should check regularly to make sure everything in her mouth is in good shape. When your vet examines your cat, he will look at her gums and choppers, but most adult cats only see their vet once or so a year; she needs more attention than that. If you do see a problem, schedule an appointment with your vet as soon as possible. He can take care of the problem or refer her to a feline dental specialist.

3. False. Cats are not big fans of "minty freshness," so your cat will not appreciate the taste in her mouth. But that's not the biggest reason to get her her own toothpaste. Read the label on your favorite tube, paying special attention to the warning "harmful if swallowed" due to fluoride toxicosis. You know not to swallow it, you can tell your kids not to, but you can't stop your cat from swallowing it, which she might do even though she hates the taste.

4. True. Just like any good behavior you want to instill in your cat, train him young. Just like using a litter box, staying off the furniture, and not scratching and biting humans, your cat will come to accept toothbrushing as part of his life.

5. True. It's likely your cat is not used to having you insert things in his mouth—unless you've ever had to give him a pill. And there's no positive association that goes along with that! However, a gum massage is a whole different story. Yes, he will be reluctant at first and wonder if you've lost your mind, but eventually, if you keep at it, he will get used to it. As soon as he accepts the intrusion and the not-unpleasant sensation of a gum massage, the more willing he'll be to at least give a try to a toothbrush.

6. False. There's no fear that cat treats will cause cavities because there's no sugar in them. Sugar is not only bad for cats, it's also useless; cats can't taste sweets, so to put a lot of sugar in a cat treat is just silly. What they do contain, however, is extra calories that your cat really doesn't need. Use good judgment: Don't spoil your cat with treats every day, but if she does something good, a treat or two makes for a great positive reward.

7. True. As odd as it sounds, one of the best times to brush your cat's teeth is before she eats. If you do this consistently, she will consider the inconvenience of having her teeth brushed minor as compared to the delight of being rewarded in her most favorite way!

8. False. If your cat sticks to a strict diet of his own cat food, it's highly unlikely he will get anything trapped in the spaces between his teeth. And, in reality, your cat has a lot more space between his teeth than the average human, making it even more unlikely that he will get food caught and require dental floss. We're afraid that fun chore is all for you to enjoy and not for kitty!

9. True. Just as it is for humans, so it is for cats. Bad oral hygiene can cause all kinds of trouble: halitosis, pain, which could lead to aggression, and periodontal disease, which could mean broken teeth or abscesses. These make eating painful—even impossible—and could lead to significant weight loss and such other health problems as infection and diseases of the heart, liver, and kidney.

10. False. Unfortunately, nature doesn't do that for anyone. If your cat has a bad tooth, it will probably have to be pulled. Check with your vet about the options available for extracting a tooth from your cat's mouth.

Give yourself a point for every correct answer. SCORE:_____

Now turn to page 217 to record your score, then head to the next quiz.

24

Pregnancy and Birth in Cats

If man could be crossed with the cat it would improve the man, but it would deteriorate the cat.
—Mark Twain

Your female cat has been starting to look a little plump in the middle lately. For the past couple of weeks or so, you've noticed that her nipples have become firmer and redder. Whether you're a breeder and you planned for this, or if you didn't realize this could happen so quickly with your unspayed cat, the verdict is the same: She's pregnant.

A mother cat typically carries anywhere from one to eight kitten fetuses, and the gestation period for kittens is about sixty-three days. During this time, and especially around the end, the mother cat has special nutritional needs. About three weeks before her kittens are due, you should start feeding your mother cat a high-quality kitten food to ensure the kittens get more protein.

Once the kittens are born, the mother cat removes the placenta, cuts their umbilical cords with her teeth, and cleans the kittens to stimulate them to breathe on their own. The new kittens begin nursing almost immediately while the mother cat eats the placenta and any evidence of their birth—an instinct not lost from the wild where the father cat has been known to eat the kittens. She will carefully look after them for the next few weeks, feeding them while also passing on vital immunities and such, and teaching them everything she knows, including how to use their litter box. Once the little ones are weaned from the mother, they will be ready to be placed in new homes of their own.

What do you know about pregnancy and birth in cats? Take the following quiz to find out.

CAT FACT

Sometimes your mother cat will ignore or overlook removing the placenta from one or more of her kittens. In that instance, the task falls to you. Call your vet right away for advice.

QUIZ #24

Answer the following multiple-choice questions to see what you really know about caring for a pregnant cat—and birthing kittens!

1. How many times a year can a female cat get pregnant.

   a. Only once
   b. About three or four times a year
   c. About seven times
   d. Twelve times—once a month

2. Which season does a female cat *not* go into heat?

   a. winter
   b. spring
   c. summer
   d. fall

3. How many male cats can father a litter?

   a. Just one.
   b. Less than two.
   c. Less than four.
   d. There can be one father for each kitten in a litter.

4. Which symptoms of pregnancy does a female cat share with humans?

   a. Morning sickness
   b. Constipation
   c. Fatigue
   d. All of the above

5. For how long is a cat typically pregnant?

   a. Four weeks
   b. Nine weeks
   c. Twenty weeks
   d. Forty weeks

6. How much weight might a female cat gain during pregnancy?

   a. Less than a pound
   b. Two to four pounds
   c. Four to six pounds
   d. As many as ten pounds, depending on the size of her litter

7. When will a cat start physically showing that she is pregnant?

   a. Right away
   b. By the end of the second week
   c. By the end of the fourth week
   d. By the end of the seventh week

8. What's the best way to help your cat give birth?

   a. Take her to the vet as soon as she's in labor.
   b. Put on a pair of surgical gloves and deliver the kittens yourself.
   c. Tear sheets and boil water.
   d. Leave her and nature to take care of the situation.

9. How soon before birth should you make a "kittening" box?

    a. As soon as you know your cat is pregnant
    b. About two months before
    c. About two weeks before
    d. Not until the cat goes into labor

10. How long will your cat typically be in labor?

    a. About six hours
    b. About ten hours
    c. About sixteen hours
    d. About twenty-six hours

Answers to Quiz #24

1. B. A female cat can get pregnant each time she goes into heat, which is about three or four times a year. Also, her gestational period is relatively short at just over two months, so pretty much as soon as she's recovered from birth and weaned her litter, she can get pregnant again fairly quickly—and likely will if you don't have her spayed. Therefore, have your female cat spayed right after her kittens are weaned.

2. A. Like most things in nature, a cat's libido is not as strong in the cold months as it is in the warm ones, so female cats generally do not go into heat in winter. But spring rolls around soon enough and look out! Your cat will be raging once the weather warms.

3. D. A litter of kittens can have as many different fathers as there are kittens; each kitten may have been sired separately.

4. D. Pregnancy is tough all around—even in the animal kingdom. While your cat could suffer all these symptoms, every pregnancy is different; sometimes she may have to endure just one or two, other times she might not be plagued with any of them.

5. B. It takes about nine weeks for a zygote, or fertilized egg, to morph into a kitten.

6. B. A pregnant cat will gain roughly two to four pounds while pregnant, or roughly 20 to 25 percent of her normal body weight.

7. C. By the end of the fourth week, the pregnant cat will start "showing" and by seven or so weeks, movement of the kittens will start to become obvious.

8. D. Cats have been giving birth for thousands of years without benefit of hospitals, doctors, or midwives. It's not necessary to take your laboring cat to the vet unless complications arise in the birth. For example, once the birthing process begins, kittens should be born every ten to sixty minutes. If more than an hour has passed since the last kitten arrived, and you know there are more, there might be an obstruction and your mother cat will need emergency medical care.

9. C. When you set up the "kittening box" about two weeks before your mother cat gives birth, it gives her an opportunity to get used to the box as a possibility for a good spot to deliver her kittens. To make a kittening box, find a good-size, shallow cardboard box and line it with shredded newspaper. Put a clean, soft towel over the paper. Place the box in a secluded area of the home that will be free of surprises and drafts. Your pregnant cat may decide to use the box, but she may have her own ideas about where she's going to give birth, so don't be offended if she doesn't accept your offer. If she's decided on another place, do not pick her up and move her to the box you made for her. Just let her be.

10. A. A healthy cat experiencing a normal pregnancy and no complications with delivery will only be in labor about six or so hours.

If her labor seems to last longer than that, call the vet as there might be complications with the delivery that he can advise you how to handle.

Give yourself a point for every correct answer. SCORE:_____

Now turn to page 217 to record your score, then head to the next quiz.

25

Breeding Cats as a Business

No man ever dared to manifest his boredom so insolently
as does a Siamese tomcat when he yawns in the face of his
amorously importunate wife.
—Aldous Huxley

B reeding cats is a serious undertaking, and all the variables need to be considered before you get started. First, there's cost: Are you willing and able to acquire enough animals so you don't overwork any? Do you have enough room to comfortably house these animals? Do you have the budget to feed and look after their medical needs? Keep in mind that cat breeding is essentially a labor of love—it will never make you wealthy. If you decide to take it on as a business, be prepared to lose some money at first, and then essentially work to recoup those losses.

The next thing to consider is time. Not only do you need enough time to see to the daily care of all these cats, but you need time for mating, looking after the special needs of pregnant mother cats, looking after the birth of the kittens, making sure the mother properly tends to her kittens, and so many other factors—including doing proper background checks on those who will be looking to acquire one of your kittens to make sure they will provide suitable homes.

Lastly, you have to be honest with yourself about whether or not you're going to be able to say good-bye to the little ones you worked so hard to bring into the world, knowing full well that once you place them in good homes, you will never see their precious little faces again.

An alternative to breeding cats as a business is breeding them for show. This also comes with many of the same time and financial constraints—and some added extras that are not relevant in breeding cats to sell, such as specialized grooming and things of that nature. Of course, because you have so much invested in these cats, you get to hold on to them and you get to avoid the sometimes painful ordeal of having to give the cats away.

So you think you know about breeding cats as a business? Take the following quiz to find out!

CAT FACT

In order to "show" your purebred cat, he must meet basic standards of his breed. If he doesn't, you won't be able to show him.

QUIZ #25

Answer the following statements True or False to see what you know about what it takes to breed cats.

1. A female cat who has not been spayed is commonly referred to as a "bitch."

2. A male breeding cat is commonly referred to as a stud.

3. Pure breed cats are typically the healthiest, most well-adjusted kinds of cats.

4. A female can produce a litter of kittens from only one male at a time.

5. Both the male and the female cat should be fully vaccinated before mating.

6. When a female cat is in heat, she is typically restless and vocal.

7. A female stays in heat, called estrus, for two weeks or more.

8. Breeding should occur in the female's first four days of estrus.

9. When mating, the male cat should be brought to the female's domain.

10. If you are breeding more than one set of cats, the nursing mothers should be allowed to hang out together and share the experience.

Answers to Quiz #25

1. False. The term used to describe a female cat ready for mating is a "queen."

2. True. You will hear this term being used for a male cat who has not been neutered and is ready to mate, along with another term: "tom." The former is more widely used in breeding circles while the latter is typically used for the male stray who hangs out in the neighborhood seeking out females to mate with.

3. False. That pure-breeding means pure everything else is a big misconception with many. Genetically speaking, the wider the mix of possible gene variables, the better the chances are of having a robust, healthy, emotionally stable cat. When all the genes come from one place in a long line of cats, all the good ones carry over from generation to generation—but so do all the bad. When the genes are so specified, there's no way to "water down" the traits that may not be desirable.

4. False. A female cat can produce a kitten from each male she mates with whiles she's in estrus. This is actually an instinctive trait passed down from female cats in the wild who would mate

with as many male cats as possible to ensure fertilization has
been successful and that the species would persevere.

5. True. For the best results with kittens, make sure both Mom
and Dad are as healthy as possible and that this good health
passes through to the kittens. It is important for females especially to be vaccinated because they will not only pass immunities
to the kitten fetuses in utero, but will continue to pass them on
while she nurses her young.

6. True. You can't confuse a cat in heat with a cat going through
any other experience. She will be restless, rambunctious, and
highly vocal, howling and screaming. She may even become more
lovey and affectionate toward you!

7. False. A non-spayed female cat can be in estrus anywhere from
three to seven days about every three weeks.

8. True. For best results, you want the cats to have enough time
to mate as many times as possible to ensure successful fertilization. If you wait too long, the sperm from the male may not reach
the female's egg in time for fertilization.

9. False. Surprisingly, mating on the male's turf is not as stressful for the female cat as mating on the female cat's turf is for
the male. The female will not feel insecure about being in his
highly territorial domain. He, on the other hand, will feel like a
fish out of water if asked to perform in a strange place, and it
could take days or even weeks before he feels comfortable mating with her.

10. False. There are no new-mother support groups in the cat
world—no Mommy and Me classes, no Gymborie. Female cats
raise their kittens on their own; for them, child rearing is a

supremely solitary experience. The presence of another cat and her kittens could actually be perceived more as a threat than anything else. So let your new mom have her privacy!

Give yourself a point for every correct answer. SCORE:_____

Now turn to page 217 to record your score, then head to the next quiz.

WHY YOUR CAT THROWS UP

Most cat lovers have worried about their cats throwing up, but most of the time when this happens, there is no cause for alarm. Persistent vomiting, however, should be checked out. Below are some of the main reasons your cat vomits:

- *Hairballs.* Perhaps the most common reason a cat will throw up is to cough up one of these irritating menaces. There are remedies out there that can help reduce the number of hairballs your cat accumulates. Ask your vet for advice.
- *Eating too much or too fast.* If your cat eats like a pig, she may not be able to digest food as quickly as it enters her system and her system will revolt. If your cat is eating too quickly, look into measures you can take to slow her down.
- *Stress.* Have you just moved? Did a new cat or other animal—or baby—just join your family? Did another animal in your family recently pass away? These are all high-stress triggers for a cat and can cause her to throw up.
- *Ingestion of a nontoxic plant.* Sometimes cats will eat plants, like grass, and the vegetation will cause the cat to throw up. With a nontoxic plant, there isn't anything to worry about; think of it as her getting her fiber, but in reverse.
- *Ingestion of a toxic plant or other toxic substance.* This is definitely cause for alarm. If your cat is vomiting because she ingested something toxic, immediately call the Animal Poison Control Center hotline at 1-888-426-4435 as well as your vet.
- *A serious illness.* The worst-case scenario for a cat that vomits is when he's suffering an illness, which means a visit to the vet. We'll look more at these possible illnesses in later chapters.

26

Traveling or Moving with Your Cat

Do you see that kitten chasing so prettily her own tail? If you could look with her eyes, you might see her surrounded with hundreds of figures performing complex dramas, with tragic and comic issues, long conversations, many characters, many ups and downs of fate.
—Ralph Waldo Emerson

If there's one thing any cat lover knows it's that cats do not like to leave their homes. Once they have their territories established, the last thing they want to do is go out and stake their claim on new turf. Mainly for this reason, traveling and especially moving can be quite taxing on your feline.

But on top of the emotional havoc, you may have many other considerations when traveling or moving with your cat. For example, what if you're making an international move? If the country you're relocating to is rabies-free, you may be forced to have your cat quarantined on premises for many months.

No matter what you do, always keep your cat in her carrier. When you fly or travel by train, this won't be an issue: No plane or train crew would permit you to let your cat roam freely through the cabin. In the car, the responsibility for keeping your cat contained lies solely on you. We can't stress this enough: Keep your cat in her carrier when you're on the road. Not only may she "mistake" your backseat for a litter box, but she may also make concentrating on the road impossible.

So what do you know about relocating with your cat on a temporary or permanent basis? Take the following quiz to find out.

CAT FACT

Home repairs and redecorating can be extremely stressful for cats, so be
sure they have a quiet, safe area to hide until the work is completed.

QUIZ #26

*Answer the following statements True or False to see if you really know what's
involved in traveling or moving with your cat.*

1. A blanket or towel full of your scent makes a great liner for a
cat carrier.

2. If your cat won't stop meowing, try taking her out of her carrier for a few minutes until she calms down.

3. If you're taking a long car trip—say for more than an hour—it's
okay to pull over regularly to let her run around the car and see if
she needs to use the litter box.

4. You should feed your cat on the day you travel with her.

5. Cat carriers now come with seat belt slots so you can strap in
your cat in the car.

6. All cats are permitted to travel in the main cabin with their humans when they travel via airplane.

7. Keeping your cat calm during air travel with a sedative or tran-
quilizer is 100 percent safe.

8. You are only required to quarantine your cat if you move or travel with your cat to another country.

9. When it comes to traveling, your best bet is to leave your cat at home.

10. When you arrive at your destination, you should let your cat sit in her carrier with the door open and let her come out when she's ready.

Answers to Quiz #26

1. True. Your cat is all about sniffing out his world, and there's no greater scent from which he derives comfort than your own. The night before you travel, try sleeping with the towel or blanket you are going to use to line your cat's carrier with. If he sleeps on it with you, all the better. The next day, when you place it in the carrier, and place him in the carrier with it, he will be much less stressed about it because he'll have those happy smells to keep him calm.

2. False. Aha! We tried to trip you up here and we were hoping you wouldn't fall for it. If you did, we're sorry to have preyed on your soft nature. If not, congratulations on remaining strong and firm. As much as your cat cries, being in her carrier is the safest place for her—and for you—in a moving car.

3. True. What's different here than the above situation is that in this instance, there is no danger—to the cat or to you. The car is pulled over and turned off and all the windows are completely shut. You aren't driving, so there's no danger of your cat jumping between you and the steering wheel—or worse yet, brake pedal—when you're trying to drive.

4. True. You don't want your cat to go hungry, but you also don't want her to have an even more miserable trip because she's suffering various digestive issues. For that reason, it's recommended that your cat be fed a small meal at least two hours prior to her being placed in her carrier. That will give the food enough time to settle.

5. True. Just as infant seats can be strapped into the backseat of your car, so can your cat's carrier. And when you think about it, doesn't it make sense? Even if you pull a shoulder-strap seatbelt over your cat's carrier, as many of us do, you're not going to get the same hold as you would if the carrier itself has special slots to be secured in the car. Check out your local pet store for these innovative models. Your cat's safety is worth it!

6. False. Don't get your hopes up on this one. Whether or not a cat will be able to travel in the main cabin with you depends on many factors, including the size of your cat and the particular airline's policies. Your best bet is to check with your airline. Keep in mind: If your cat meets the airline's requirements for cabin travel, you will need to purchase a specialized airline-approved carrier that will tuck under the seat in front of you.

7. False. As with any medication, your cat may have a reaction to the sedative you give her prior to air travel. If she's in the cabin with you, you can look out for her. If she's in the cargo hold, you're not going to know anything's wrong until you pick her up after the flight. For that reason, you should go over with your vet all the risks and benefits of sedating your cat before traveling. The best bet for your cat, especially if the trip you're taking isn't very long, may just be to not sedate her.

8. False. The quarantine rule applies anywhere that's been proven to be rabies-free. There are only a few countries absolutely proven to be rabies-free, such as Australia, the British Isles, and New Zealand. However, since 2002, the quarantine rule has not applied to properly vaccinated animals coming into Great Britain. When traveling within the United States, Hawaii requires a quarantine period of 130 days. For more information on pet quarantine rules and regulations, visit a pet-travel website such as petsonthego.com, or call the travel and tourism office of the location you are looking to visit or relocate to.

9. True. As we've already stated, cats are not ambitious travelers. They harbor no deep-seated desires to get out and see the world. A cat is content with the world of her own home, where she knows where to find her food and water, her litter box, and where she's already found all the best hiding places. For these reasons, it's best to leave your cat home when you travel. Ask a neighbor or friend to look in on her daily—not only to make sure her food bowl is full and her water fresh, but also to give her those strokes and pats she so eagerly craves. Moving is a different story: Of course you'd never leave your cat behind unless you absolutely could not take her with you. In this case, it's important to put finding her a good home at the top of your moving "to-do" list.

10. True. We can't say it enough: Being taken away from her familiar environment is about as stressful an event as a cat will ever endure. Let her enjoy the safety and security of her carrier for as long as she needs. Eventually, the call for food and litter will take over, her natural curiosity will overtake her apprehension, and she will be ready to stake a claim on her brave new world.

Give yourself a point for every correct answer. SCORE:_____

Now turn to page 217 to record your score, then head to the next quiz.

27

Separation Anxiety

What greater gift than the love of a cat?
—Charles Dickens

Contrary to what many think—that cats are completely independent spirits who are much happier to be by themselves than be burdened with having to entertain humans or even other cats—domestic cats are actually very social animals. They can become quite lonely if left to themselves for too long. That's why it's always recommended that you have more than one cat, especially if you aren't home a lot.

You think we have it bad when it comes to devotion to our feline friends? Well, cats become extremely attached to their humans. Have you ever come home to find your laundry hamper turned over? What about those missing socks you blame on the annoying antics of the dryer fairy? Why do you suppose that insufferable imp has decided to hide that sock under your bed or in the back of your closet? Answer: There is no dryer fairy. Your cat, to be close to you, might just run off with one of your used articles of clothing from time to time. After all, where else is your scent stronger?

How much do you know about how much your cat likes to have you around? Take the following quiz to see.

CAT FAOT

A microchip with identification can be painlessly embedded in your cat in case she is ever lost or stolen.

QUIZ #27

Answer the following statements True or False to see what you know about cats and separation anxiety.

1. Most cats don't notice you've been gone until you return home.

2. Playing soothing classical music for your cat while you're gone during the day will keep him calm and relaxed.

3. While some may feel it and express it more intensely, all cats experience separation anxiety.

4. Before you leave the house, it's a good idea to kiss and hug and say good-bye to your cat as much as possible. It will reassure her.

5. While you're out, you should call your cat every time the mood strikes and talk on your own answering machine so he can hear your voice as often as possible. It will make him think you're still home.

6. If you leave a picture of yourself by your cat's bed, she will be comforted by it.

7. If you have to go out of town for a few days, you should board your cat.

8. Your cat may express his displeasure at your absence by leaving you a "gift" of his own making in your bed, bathtub, or other inappropriate spot.

9. If you have a particularly needy cat, you should talk to your boss about taking your cat to work with you. It will be in everyone's best interests.

10. If you're away from home a lot, your best alternative is to give your cat away.

Answers to Quiz #27

1. False. There's a common misconception that cats will spend the entire time their humans are away sleeping, but this is not true. For one, cats, by nature, sleep in spurts. Even if they sleep most of the time, they do get up to stretch, play, eat, drink, and use their litter boxes while you're away. Time doesn't conveniently stop for them. So while they may not fully comprehend in hours or minutes how long you've been away, anyone who's been greeted—and even scolded—by their cat at the front door knows that their cat is well aware that they haven't been around.

2. True. Classical music has been known to calm cats while their owners are away. Simply put, your cat likes the background noise. Even though she knows it's not you making the sounds, she still derives comfort from it. That said, if you do leave a radio on during the day for your cat, make sure you're tuned into a soothing classical music station; hard rock and heavy metal will not have the same soothing effect.

3. True. Think your cat doesn't care whether you live or die? Don't worry. Your cat does love you, no matter how she behaves with you. Believe it or not, even the most "antisocial" of cats craves the presence of her human, even if she won't admit it to you by actually being just where you are or jumping into your lap every time you happen to be sitting down. For some cats, as long as she's in earshot of you, she will be happy. If you're not around, a less affectionate cat will actually miss you just as much as the most affectionate one. She might just have different ways to show you, as we'll see later in this chapter.

4. False. As hard as this may be to wrap your brain around, your cat actually experiences deeper separation anxiety when you emphasize that you're leaving and remind him several times by giving him more than the usual doses of affection and attention. So as hard as it may be, try to resist the urge to smother your cat with love when you have to leave him, whether you're running a few short errands, going to work, or heading off on vacation. Believe it or not, this will actually be better for him.

5. False. Just as you shouldn't smother your cat with love before you leave her, you should not constantly call her during the day to remind her that you're not around. For one, cats generally startle when they hear a phone ring. And while she will likely recognize your voice coming from the machine, she will probably connect less with the fact that you're calling to check in with her than that the darn phone won't stop ringing. Once in a while, like if you're away for a week or so, give a call. Otherwise, just leave her be. You'll be seeing her soon enough!

6. False. As much as she may love you, your cat is simply not as sentimental as you are. Therefore, a picture of you by her bed is not going to warm her heart as much as a picture of her in your office or cubicle warms yours. Besides, your cat associates you more with your scent than your looks. Instead of a photo, leave her a shirt that you wore or a towel you dried off with. These will be much more significant to her.

7. False. We can't emphasize enough that your cat finds leaving his own environment among the most stressful events of his life. So if

you have to go out of town for a few days—or even a few weeks—
you should do whatever you can to avoid having to board your cat.
Your going away is traumatic enough for your little friend, so your
best bet is to at least let her stay at home in comfortable surroundings and have a friend or relative look in on her. If you absolutely,
positively have no choice but to board your cat, be sure to pack her
up with her favorite cat food and an article of clothing with your
scent on it to minimize stress.

8. True. Your cat may have a thousand meows in her vocabulary,
but she knows the best way to make a point with you is not with
"words," but with actions. If your cat pees or poops outside her litter box, it usually means something's wrong with her—and not necessarily physically wrong. Notice that your cat will not "miss" the
box while you're away; she waits until you come back. This is because it's important for her to let you know exactly how unhappy
she was to have been left alone like that, and if she does it while
you're away, you may not get the message because these little
"hints" tend to dry out over time and become less effective.

9. False. If you answered True to this question, clearly this is the
first question you answered in this book! Not only does your cat
want to be home where all her luscious smells and hiding places are,
your boss and coworkers do not want your cat roaming around the
office. Some of your colleagues may have allergies or other cat issues, and some may find her ridiculously cute, therefore inhibiting
them from focusing on their jobs. The only one who will be happy
is you—but try and make this be not so much about you, okay?

10. False. In any situation, giving your cat away should be the last
possible resort. Adopting a cat is a responsibility you take on for
life. If your cat does get desperately lonely, consider the alternatives. Maybe you have a retired neighbor who would relish hanging
out in your place a half an hour or so a day playing with your cat.
There are also cat-sitting services that can provide company for

your cat at nominal costs. And don't overlook the obvious: another cat. Sure, the introduction process may be trying, but once cats take to one another, they can make great company for each other — even doing things together you can't, like grooming each other. Remember, before you decide to give a cat away, please consider all possible alternatives. If you think you're leaving a few hours during the day is traumatic for your cat, consider how bad it will be for her to never see you again.

Give yourself a point for every correct answer. SCORE:_____

Now turn to page 217 to record your score, then head to the next quiz.

28

Dealing with Aggressive Behavior

The great charm of cats is their rampant egotism, their
devil-may-care attitude toward responsibility, their disin-
clination to earn an honest dollar.
—Robertson Davies

Aggressive behavior is a fact of nature and occurs in every species on the globe. Some species, however, are more aggressive than others, and our furry friends, the fabulous felines, have been known to make high marks in this category. Even the most docile cat, if provoked, will present his inner lion.

The good news is that aggressive behavior in a domestic cat is typically reactionary. Sure, some cats have a hereditary predisposition to aggressive behavior, but in many, this type of behavior is sparked by fear, desire to protect territory, illness or discomfort, and other external factors.

Whatever the cause, getting your cat's aggressive behavior under control is essential. If you don't your cat may believe it's perfectly within her rights to bite or scratch you—or, even worse, other adults and naturally curious and rambunctious children who may come for a visit. You don't want your guests leaving your home with the words "lawsuit" on the brain.

How much do you know about cats and aggressive behavior? Take the following quiz to find out!

CAT FACT

Cats are creatures of habit, so a cat faced with too many unpredictable elements in his life will not be a very happy cat.

QUIZ #28

Answer the following multiple-choice questions to see if you know how to handle an aggressive cat.

1. An aggressive cat:

   a. Is just born that way
   b. Is usually provoked to aggression
   c. Is incurable
   d. Must be put down so he won't hurt anyone

2. You adopted a naturally aggressive cat because you felt that no one else would and you felt sorry for him. When you get him home, you:

   a. Lock him in a room and keep him there always.
   b. Let him dominate you—it's in his nature after all.
   c. Begin a training regimen to help curb his aggressive behavior.
   d. Realize you made a grave error in judgment and return him to the shelter the following day.

3. If your cat has just undergone a traumatic experience, you should:

   a. Smother her with hugs and kisses so she knows how much you care.
   b. Locate her hiding spot and check in on her every fifteen minutes or so.
   c. Leave her alone and let her come to you for comfort when she's ready.
   d. Board her at the vet's office overnight so she can have some peace and quiet.

4. Your cat has just had a nasty altercation with the dog. You should:

  a. Put the two together so they can make up.
  b. Keep them separated for a while until tempers cool.
  c. Give the dog away.
  d. Have the dog put down.

  5. You have two cats and one seems to dominate the other. You should:

  a. Gang up with your submissive cat against your dominant cat and see how he likes being bullied.
  b. Punish your dominant cat every time you catch him pushing his weight around.
  c. Bring your submissive cat to therapy to teach her about empowerment.
  d. Accept that this is natural behavior for cats who find themselves having to share territory.

  6. Your cat is typically not aggressive, but for some reason, he likes to bite and scratch at your ankles. Do you . . . ?

  a. Indulge his behavior, as you and he both know he means no harm.
  b. Distract him with a less obnoxious activity.
  c. Yell loudly at him to let him know it's not okay to bite and scratch you.
  d. Bite and scratch him back. He'll see it's not that much fun when he's the recipient and he'll learn to leave you alone.

7. Your cat has just had a litter of kittens. Do you   ?

   a. Jump right in and help her with her maternal responsibilities—she'll appreciate the gesture!
   b. Watch over her at all times and make sure she takes proper care of them.
   c. Keep an eye on her, but from a distance.
   d. Ignore her and her kittens for at least three weeks. Nature has given her the wherewithal to take care of her young and you have no place in that picture.

8. Which of the following is a sure warning sign that a fearful cat is about to lash out:

   a. His ears go flat.
   b. His tail lashes.
   c. His eyes blink furiously.
   d. His back arches.

9. If your friend visits with her feisty five-year-old, and the boy seems much more interested in your cat than she seems in him, you should:

   a. Let him stalk her out and make friends with her.
   b. Bring your cat out into the living room and make sure she can't retreat to another room so you can keep your eye on them.
   c. Lock her in a room with the curious child so they can get acquainted without the pressure of "parents" watching over them.
   d. Ask your friend to instruct her child to leave the cat alone.

10. If you can't get your cat's aggression under control, your best bet is to:

    a. Just work around her behavior and hope one day she will change.

    b. Talk to your vet about possible drug-therapy treatments.

    c. Drop her off on the doorstep of a neighbor you dislike.

    d. Take her to the vet and have her put to sleep.

Answers to Quiz #28

1. B. While it is true that some cats are aggressive by nature, the majority of cats will exhibit aggressive behavior primarily only when provoked. Even a cat born with aggressive tendencies can be reformed, however, with consistent training. Whether you have that kind of time and patience is what will determine if the cat can be changed. The option of putting an overly aggressive cat down is a very last resort.

2. C. A naturally aggressive cat may try to dominate you if left to his own devices. When this occurs, you have to let him know who's boss. Assert your position as the "alpha cat" in your household from the beginning through gentle, consistent discipline—gentle and consistent being the key words here. If you react angrily and aggressively to your cat's aggressive behavior, you could actually end up making the problem worse.

3. C. If your cat has been traumatized, try to give her as much space as you possibly can. She needs time to calm down, and if you push her before she's ready, handling her or even stalking her without touching her, she might just lash out at you. But whatever you do, don't drag her off to the hospital unless she's injured. The best place for her to get a grip is on her own turf with her own smells.

4. B. Exactly how long you keep them separated depends on the degree of the altercation and the nature of both animals. Don't be so quick to punish the dog because your cat, angel that she is, may have provoked the attack. Your best bet when it comes to living with cats and dogs is to supervise all interactions.

5. D. You can take the cat out of the wild, but you can't take the wild out of the cat. It is in the feline nature to establish hierarchies of dominancy, and your domestic cats are no exception. Your interference in this is not going to change anything; all it could do possibly is upset the natural balance that both cats are perfectly content with.

6. B. As stated above, your cat will push the limits and try to get away with whatever he feels like getting away with. It's your job to curb his behavior. That said, he will not respond well to retaliation or loud reprimands. The best way out of all these options to make him stop doing something obnoxious is to entice him with a much more tolerable activity.

7. C. While it is true that nature has equipped the female cat with the instincts to look after her young, sometimes she may fall down on the job. For that reason, you should look in on her from time to time. Anything more than that, however, will not only be considered an intrusion but a flat-out threat to her and her kittens. Get too close to a mother cat nurturing her kittens and you'll get a healthy dose — likely in the form of a nasty scratch or bite — of what it means for a mother cat to be protective of her babies. Even the most docile cat is prone to aggression when it comes to this particular circumstance.

8. A, B, and D are all correct. If you answered any of these, give yourself a point. Excessive blinking is not something a cat ever does (even when he blinks love signals to you, it's done slowly and rhythmically) unless he's gotten something in his eyes. So sorry, if you answered C, no point for you!

9. D. A curious and rambunctious child can be public enemy number one for even the most outgoing cat. If your cat shows her lack of interest in the child, don't force her to accept him. You'll only be asking for trouble. And while you may have a cranky preschooler on your hands temporarily, his mother will understand.

10. B. You don't want to just deal with an aggressive cat; nor should you abandon her to someone else or worse. If your careful discipline has not worked, your cat may be a candidate for drug therapy. Speak to your vet about the options available.

Give yourself a point for every correct answer. SCORE:_____

Now turn to page 217 to record your score, then head to the next quiz.

Name: Brownie
Humans: The Rosen Family

Name: Brittany
Humans: The Rosen Family

Name: Sabrina
Humans: The Rosen Family

Name: Cody   Humans: The Rosen Family

Name: Mario   Human: Zan Farr

Name: Will
Humans: The Rosen Family

Name: Lily
Humans: The Rosen Family

Name: Reggie
Human: Zan Farr

Name: McGee
Human: Zan Farr

Name: Marcie
Human: Zan Farr

Name: Daisy   Human: Deanna Parsi

Name: Carlotta
Human: Anne Brooks

Name: Maggie
Humans: Stephanie and Rupert
    Ruding-Bryan

Name: Emma Jane   Human: Deanna Parsi

Names: Simon *(left)* and Todd
Humans: The Hornberger Family
Comment: All the news that's fit to poop on.

Name: Emma
Human: Cheryl Hackert

Names: Sampson (*left*) and Mitzy   Human: Maria Tahim

Name: Gracie
Humans: The Mayer Family

Name: Ajax
Humans: Mindy and Pete Walker

Name: Cheech
Human: Michele Santelices
Comment: "Is it time for *Desperate Housecats*?"

Name: Josie
Humans: The LaSala Family
Comment: "Christmas. Big whoop."

Name: Fluffy
Humans: The LaSala Family

Name: Snowy
Humans: Ian and Karen Chow-Miller

Name: Moots
Human: Colette Carey

Name: Cosmo
Human: Nicole Dauenhauer

Name: Monroe
Humans: Jennifer and Don Ridd«

Name: Frankie Pink Nose
Humans: "Who wants to know?"
Comment: "You gotta problem
with my name?"

Name: Cosmo   Human: Lucille Collins

29

Cat Characteristics III

I wish I could write as mysterious as a cat.
—Edgar Allan Poe

You've made it all the way to the third part of the Cat Characteristics quiz—congratulations! When it comes to cats and their unique characteristics, well, let's just say there could be a quiz book on that topic alone!

In the first quiz, we looked at basic cat characteristics, like what their whiskers are for, how many teeth they have, and how well they see and hear. The second quiz was a little more challenging, examining certain genetic traits and what they mean for your cat as well as how to interpret her mood by observing the size of her pupils and more. This quiz, although it contains some general information, will ask the most obscure questions about cat characteristics.

Are you up for the challenge? Take the following quiz to see!

CAT FACT
Toilet water may contain a variety of harmful bacteria and treatment chemicals, which your cat will find irresistible—so keep the lid down!

QUIZ #29

Answer the following questions True or False to see how much more you know about cat characteristics.

1. The hairs on your cat's body stand erect only when she is angry.

2. A cat sheds for more reasons than just changing its coat.

3. When a cat lays on her back with her paws in the air, exposing her stomach, it means she feels secure.

4. A cat's heart beats at close to the same pace as a human heart.

5. Because cats hate the water, except for drinking, no cat can swim.

6. Cats dream when they sleep.

7. Cats have extra tissue in the larynx, which vibrates when they purr.

8. Cats lose more fluid by grooming themselves than they do expelling urine.

9. Your cat has an extra pad on each of her front legs that isn't used for walking.

10. Cats can have freckles.

Answers to Quiz #29

1. False. While the hairs on your kitty's coat will bristle when she's angry and ready to tussle, fear will also cause her hair to stand erect. If your cat's coat is standing at end, take this as a sure signal to keep away.

2. True. Your cat will shed his coat the most when the weather turns from cold to warm and he needs less insulation, but the shed instinct can also be triggered by light exposure. For this reason, cats who are strictly indoor may shed more than outdoor cats because they are constantly exposed to artificial light. A cat will also shed if he is stressed out or ill. If your cat seems to be losing a lot of hair lately, and it's not weather-related, make an appointment with your vet to ensure he's in good physical and mental health.

3. False. Although a cat laying on her back with her paws down is the sign of a happy, secure cat, when her paws are extended upward in this position, it actually means she's ready to fight. This posture seems submissive; however, a cat has a lot of power on her back and can do a lot of damage to an attacker, especially with her back legs.

4. False. The speed of a heart in any living thing depends on the size of the living thing being kept alive by the heart. Typically, smaller animals have faster heartbeats than larger ones. Your cat's heart beats about 120 to 200 times a minute on average, while a typical human heart rate is about 70 beats per minute.

5. False. Interestingly enough, all cats—including the big, wild relatives of your domestic cat—can swim. This doesn't mean they like to, of course, so don't toss your cat in the pool to test it out. After paddling her way back to dry land, it's likely she will never speak to you again.

6. True. Cats do dream when they sleep, but like their human friends, this dreaming only occurs in the deep phases of their sleep. Have you ever watched your cat sleep peacefully and then all of a sudden her ears and paws start to twitch? This is a sign that your cat is dreaming. Sometimes she may even "talk" in her sleep, vocalizing as she twitches. Exactly what does your cat dream about? Like us, a cat processes the information she's taken in during the day, at random, so it's likely she's dreaming of you, or her kibble, or playing with her cat friends, or even of a bird she may have spotted from a window.

7. True. Cats are the only animals who purr, and all cats do it, from the king of the jungle to the king of your household. There are several theories as to how and why cats purr, though it is not completely certain if purring is a voluntary or involuntary act. One theory as to how cats purr states that purring occurs through the vibration of two extra flaps of tissue in the larynx behind the vocal cords. Another is that purring is caused by vibrations through major blood vessels in the chest. Interesting to note: Purring is how kittens and mama cats communicate. As the newborn kittens are both blind and deaf, they can find their mother through the vibrations of her purr, and also communicate back to her through the same method.

8. False. Cats may not lose as much fluid grooming as they do through urination, but with all the time they spend cleaning themselves and all the saliva they use, it's pretty darn close!

9. True. This pad, called the accessory carpal pad, isn't used for walking. Look at it—it's much too high! Rather, this pad is there almost as a brake. As your cat leaps and bounds around your house at ninety miles an hour, she uses that pad to keep her from skidding.

10. True. Believe it or not, your cat could be hiding freckles under her coat. While sometimes a cat may have a freckle or two on her nose, they usually appear under the coat and even in her mouth. And here's an interesting bit of big cat trivia: Did you know that tigers have stripped skin under their striped coats? It's absolutely true!

Give yourself a point for every correct answer. SCORE:_____

Now turn to page 217 to record your score, then head to the next quiz.

CATNIP

Few things are more hilarious than a cat that's had a dose of catnip. While a small percentage of cats won't feel any reaction to the slightly hallucinogenic herb, most will react basically by acting like a nut job. Cats love to rub their faces in the stuff and will generally be more hyper than even their typical selves. The effect only lasts about fifteen minutes or so. Got questions about catnip? Some common ones are answered below.

What is catnip?
Catnip, sometimes called "cat mint," is one of the herbs in the mint family.

How does it work?
Catnip contains nepetalactone, a substance thought to have a mild but safe hallucinogenic effect on cats. Not only domestic cats are affected by it, but also wild cats like bobcats, lions, tigers, and others have a penchant for the plant. It is interesting to note that the cat gets his thrill from the smell of the herb and not the taste. It is rarely, if ever, ingested by the cat.

How much catnip should cats have?
A little goes a long way. About half a teaspoon of the stuff should be enough to affect your cat.

Is there such a thing as too much catnip?
Just as with anything, a cat can have too much catnip. It's not particularly harmful per se. She won't have a psychotic split or anything like that, but too much could cause your cat some uncomfortable vomiting or diarrhea.

When will cats not react to catnip?
Some cats, about one in five, just don't react to the stuff. There's really no scientific explanation why. One thing that is known is that catnip is not for the little ones. While it will not harm them, kittens under the age of six months will probably have no reaction to catnip.

Will catnip affect me the same way it does my cat?
No, it really only affects cats. Of course, if you don't believe us, go ahead and rub your face in some to see what happens! Humans have been known to use catnip, but for medicinal and not party purposes. Catnip teas are sometimes prescribed by herbalists as a remedy for colds, flu, and other human ailments.

Can I grow my own catnip?
As catnip is an herb, yes, you can grow it (and legally). For best results, plant catnip seeds in a sunny location in the early spring. If you live in a place where the winters are not too harsh, the same plants will sprout every year.

30

Preventive Health Care for Cats

I love cats because I enjoy my home; and little by little,
they become its visible soul.
—Jean Cocteau

Just like it is with the human members of your family, so it is with your felines: The best way to control illness is to prevent it before it has a chance to bring itself on. A cat who is brought to the vet for regular checkups and whose humans keep vigilant about his overall health and well-being will be much less susceptible to sickness than a cat who isn't regularly monitored. With the exception of a handful of conditions that cannot be avoided because they are hereditary, and accidents that are known to happen even under the most cat-conscious circumstances, the state of your cat's health rests in your hands. Are you up to the task?

Take the following quiz and see how much you know about preventive health care for your cat.

CAT FACT

Cats share many of the same allergies as humans, including insect bites, medications, and certain foods.

QUIZ #30

Answer the following statements True or False to see what you know about keeping your cat healthy.

1. Your adult cat should visit the vet at least once a year.

2. Vaccinations are required only once in your cat's life.

3. Your vet should do little more than weigh your cat and check her heartbeat when you bring your cat to visit him.

4. Spaying or neutering your kitten will prolong his or her health and life.

5. If your cat gets fleas, you won't need to do anything more than treat her with a flea shampoo and a flea collar, which will prevent the pesky critters from coming back.

6. You should take a stray in only after you've brought her to the vet for inspection and blood work and everything checks out.

7. No harm will come to your cat if you smoke around him.

8. It's not your responsibility to keep records of your cat's health. A good vet will take care of this for you.

9. Your cat should be permitted to run around outdoors.

10. You should never hit your cat, but if you need to make a serious point with him, shaking him is okay.

Answers to Quiz #30

1. True. Just as humans should have yearly physicals, so should cats. Even if your cat seems healthy, vibrant, and strong, you should make sure everything's okay with her.

2. False. Once given, vaccinations need to be followed up with booster shots every so often, depending on the vaccination.

3. False. If this is all your vet does when you bring your cat in for a checkup, you should seriously consider seeing another vet. Your vet should first take a complete medical history. In addition to weighing your cat and checking her heart rate, your vet should listen to your cat's lungs. He should inspect your cat's body from head to tail, searching out any abnormalities such as lumps, bumps, scrapes, swelling, parasites, abscesses, and more. He should also check for any unusual discharge as well as inspect her teeth and gums, and make recommendations for blood tests and other types of tests when appropriate.

4. True. As we covered in the chapter on spaying or neutering your cat, spaying your female will protect her from developing various cancers, whereas neutering your male will, among other benefits, keep him from getting himself into deadly trouble by acting in an overly assertive manner with another animal who might decide to rend him to shreds for his behavior.

5. False. What most people don't realize about the insidious wee beasties commonly known as fleas is just how insidious they are. Your cat can get fleas from another animal, which is the most common way, but she can also pick them up from being in an environment where they reside. That's right: Fleas do not have to hang out in the coat of a cat or a dog to survive. So if your cat had fleas, and you treated her with a shampoo and flea collar and called it a day, you didn't do enough. Even if you went a step farther than a flea collar, using one of the more sophisticated topical spot treatments available through your vet—which safely kill and repel fleas for a month at a time—it isn't enough. To ensure these pests don't come back, you actually need to fumigate your entire home. Just be careful: The chemicals in pest poisons are toxic. Read labels. It may be a good idea to relocate your cat to a flea-free environment for a couple of days while you fumigate.

6. True. As we talked about earlier in the chapter on adopting a cat, strays can be riddled with parasites and disease. This is not something you want to expose your existing cat to. If you're planning to take in a stray, you must first take him to the vet to make sure he is disease- and parasite-free, and also to have him altered if he isn't already. Be sure he gets any treatments he needs to cure any illness, and make sure he has a 100 percent clean bill of health before letting him anywhere near your cat.

7. False. Just like humans, cats are susceptible to the dangers of second-hand smoke, including lung cancer, so if you really need to light up, why not do your innocent smoke-free cat a favor and take it outside?

8. False. Even if you have the best vet in the world, you should always keep your own records of your cat's health. The reason for this is that you don't take your cat to the vet every time she has diarrhea or vomits, falls, gets scraped up, or what have you. Therefore, the only way to have your cat's health history fully recorded is to take it down and file it for yourself.

9. False. The more time a cat spends outdoors, the more susceptible he becomes to contracting parasites, catching illnesses, getting hit by cars, and fighting with other cats—or other animals like dogs or even raccoons. Want to keep your cat safe and healthy? Keep him in a controlled environment—indoors!

10. False. Just as it is with a baby, shaking a cat can actually do more damage to the animal than simply hitting a cat—and you should do neither. Ever. If your cat misbehaves, squirt him with a water bottle. Make a loud noise—even clap. But never lay a hand on him.

Give yourself a point for every correct answer. SCORE:_____

Now turn to page 217 to record your score, then head to the next quiz.

31

Caring for an Older Cat

It doesn't do to be sentimental about cats; the best ones
don't respect you for it.
—Susan Howatch

These days, cats are living longer than ever and many are known to stay in excellent health throughout their golden years. However, as healthy as your senior cat may be, her body is beginning to slow itself down. Her hearing and eyesight become less sharp, her coat may thin out, her skin may become flaky, and she may even gain a few extra pounds. Of course, these are just a handful of the changes in store for your cat as her life progresses.

Although all this is normal, there are many ways you can ensure your older cat stays in top health, and make her as comfortable and joyful as a kitten as she enjoys her later years.

So you think you know what it takes to make your older cat happy? Take the following quiz to find out.

CAT FACT

Cats who live in stimulating environments are much better equipped for losing the keenness of their senses in old age.

QUIZ #31

Answer the following statements True or False to see what you know about taking care of your older cat.

1. A cat will start showing signs of aging at about seven years old, and steadily deteriorate from that point on.

2. Your older cat will gleefully welcome a youngster into his life.

3. You should feed your older cat smaller, more frequent meals.

4. You should not switch your cat over to senior cat food until she is at least eleven years old.

5. Your older cat may lose some of her teeth.

6. Older cats can sleep more than kittens.

7. Your older cat should visit her vet more frequently than once a year.

8. As your cat ages, her hearing and vision will gradually decrease.

9. Older cats typically lose all interest in playtime.

10. As your cat gets older, she will start becoming despondent and depressed, always yearning for her younger days.

Answers to Quiz #31

1. False. When it comes to aging, cats are really tricky. For the most part, a cat will barely show signs of aging for years while she's a senior; it's more of an "all of a sudden" situation. In other words, a fourteen-year-old cat could easily pass for a four-year-old. It's only when the signs of aging begin to show that you realize your cat is not a kitten anymore.

2. False. By the time he's a senior, your older cat has his routine and his life just the way he likes it and has little need for making new friends at this point in his life. Keep in mind that a younger cat may be overcome with joy at having a playmate to mess around with, and might pounce at, bat, or even chase the tail of your old guy when he's not in the mood to be played with. This could lead to aggressive behavior on the old man's part—and a nasty scratch or welt on the curious newcomer. Generally speaking, you should hold off bringing another cat home if your old cat is more than fourteen years old.

3. True. Just like most everything else, your older cat's metabolism is slowing down. If he eats too much at once, he might not be able to properly work off the calories, which will result in weight gain. Also, his digestive system is not as efficient as it used to be, and the less food he eats at a sitting, the less chance there is he'll develop any kind of gastrointestinal upset.

4. False. Though cats are not typically classified as seniors until they are about ten or eleven years old, it is generally recommended that a cat be started on a senior food diet when she hits middle age. Her metabolism is not as slow as an older cat at that time, but it's not quite functioning at the kitten rate either. By feeding her a reduced-calorie, reduced-fat senior formula, you will decrease the chances that she will become obese.

5. True. Just as humans lose their teeth when old age creeps in, so do cats. To ensure your cat keep as many teeth as she can for as long as she can, be sure to be vigilant about her oral hygiene. After all, there is no such thing as kitty dentures—and have you ever met a cat who would ever deign to wear them if there were?!

6. True. Older cats are sleepy cats and can be known to rest their eyes upward of seventeen hours a day!

7. True. As your cat gets older, the chances that she could develop life-threatening diseases including renal failure, diabetes, and heart and liver disease, as well as conditions like cataracts, sharply increase. An older cat should see her vet at least twice a year.

8. True. Just like in humans, the senses dull the older a cat gets. Gradual hearing loss is common in aging cats, as well as is vision loss, decreased agility, decreased muscle mass, slowed reaction times, a less efficient circulatory and pulmonary system, and diminished immunity. Older cats are also susceptible to tumors, thyroid disease, constipation, arthritis, and more—making an even stronger case for that bi-yearly visit to the vet!

9. False. Older cats are essentially kittens at heart. While you won't generally see your older cat taking over at ninety miles an hour to chase a phantom intruder that no one else sees down the hall, you certainly can entice her to bat—however lazily—at a catnip mouse tied to a string.

10. False. Unlike humans, cats are not programmed with regret— nor are they particularly interested in yesterday or tomorrow. If your cat seems despondent, it likely has nothing to do with being sad about not having the same robust energy and drive she once enjoyed; she's probably just tired and bored in the moment she happens to be living. Chances are, she'll soon get bored of being bored and her mood will change with the wind. (Note: If your cat has been experiencing extreme, consistent lethargy, it may be a sign that something is physically wrong. Make an appointment with your vet.)

Give yourself a point for every correct answer. SCORE:_____

Now turn to page 217 to record your score, then head to the next quiz.

32

Cats in Art

*There's no need for a piece of sculpture in a home that has
a cat.*
—Wesley Bates

T he poet and artist Jean Cocteau was so devoted to his cat,
Karoun, that Karoun actually wore a collar that said "Cocteau
belongs to me." This level of devotion is not unusual for artistic
and creative types throughout the ages. There's just something so
magical, so mystical about the feline species. They are walking,
breathing, purring manifestations of inspiration, and have been cel-
ebrated in art, literature, and more because of this.

We'll look at famous cats in literature in Chapter 37. This chapter looks at cats as they appear in the works of some of the great
masters of art. If you don't know anything about art, you may find
this to be one of the more challenging quizzes in the book; however, if you do well, you can impress cat-loving friends and ac-
quaintances at cocktail parties for years to come!

So you think you know about cats as they have appeared in art
throughout the ages? Take the quiz on the following pages to see
how much you really know!

CAT FACT

Your cat sweats even though she has no sweat glands. While she regulates heat mostly through grooming, she does perspire through the pads on her feet!

QUIZ #32

Match up these columns of famous artists with the cat art works for which they are known.

1. Marc Chagall
2. Paul Klee
3. Henri Matisse
4. Pablo Picasso
5. Andy Warhol
6. Théophile Alexandre Steinlen
7. Pierre Auguste Renoir
8. Marc Franz
9. Fernando Botero
10. Leonardo da Vinci

a. *Wounded Bird and Cat* (1938)
b. *Three Cats* (1913)
c. *The Cat Transformed into a Woman* (1927–1930)
d. *Study of a Child with a Cat* (1478)
e. *Girl with a Black Cat* (1910)
f. *Girl and Cat* (1881)
g. *Le Chat Noir* (1881)
h. *Cat on a Roof* (1978)
i. *Cat and Bird* (1928)
j. *A Cat Named Sam* (1970)

Answers to Quiz #32

1. C. Marc Chagall painted *The Cat Transformed into a Woman.*

2. E. Paul Klee painted *Girl with a Black Cat.*

3. I. Henri Matisse painted *Cat and Bird.*

4. A. Pablo Picasso painted *Wounded Bird and Cat.*

5. J. Andy Warhol painted *A Cat Named Sam.*
6. G. Théophile Alexandre Steinlen painted *Le Chat Noir.*

7. F. Pierre Auguste Renoir painted *Girl and Cat.*

8. B. Marc Franz painted *Two Cats.*

9. H. Fernando Botero painted *Cat on a Roof.*

10. D. Leonardo da Vinci did the *Study of a Child with a Cat.*

Give yourself a point for every correct answer. SCORE:_____

Now turn to page 217 to record your score, then head to the next quiz.

33

First Aid and Emergency Care for Your Cat

How we behave toward cats here below determines our
status in heaven.
—Robert A. Heinlein

Your cat deserves only the best from you, so as a good cat human, you should know everything there is to know about taking care of your cat. This goes far past the typical day-to-day maintenance of feeding, watering, grooming, and litter box upkeep, however. Your cat needs to be able to count on you in any situation.

It is extremely important for cat humans to know as much as they can about things that are not part of the daily routine, including first aid and emergency care. Your cat can't take herself to the vet if she's in distress; she can't bandage a wound by herself or even soothe a burn. These are things she relies on you for—and things you need to be up to the task for should the call ever arise.

If, God forbid, your cat does get injured—seriously or not—you must maintain a cool, collected head. Never panic, because not only will you be inefficient in her care, you might also seriously freak her out if you go nuts. Be sure to learn everything you can about first aid and emergency care so you can be there for your cat when she needs you the most.

So will you know how to jump to action if your cat has a medical emergency? Take the following quiz to find out.

CAT FACT

Cats who live in smokers' households have a significantly increased risk of developing lung cancer.

QUIZ #33

Answer the following multiple-choice questions to see what you know about kitty first aid.

1. If your cat gets a minor cut or scrape:

    a. Just ignore it. These things happen.
    b. Clean the wound with an antibacterial soap and clean water or hydrogen peroxide and otherwise leave it alone unless it starts to bleed or pus.
    c. Clean the wound with a disinfectant ointment and always wrap the affected area in a bandage.
    d. Rush her to your vet's office. You can never be too careful!

2. To properly take your cat's temperature, you must place the thermometer:

    a. In her mouth
    b. In her ear
    c. Under one of her front legs
    d. In her anus

3. Where's the best place to take your cat's pulse?

    a. Just above the pads of her front paws
    b. On her neck
    c. On her tummy
    d. On the inside of one of her rear legs

4. Which of the following should you have in a first-aid kit for your cat?

   a. Tweezers
   b. Disinfectant ointment
   c. Gauze bandages
   d. Petroleum jelly

5. If one of your cat's limbs appears to be broken, you should:

   a. Thrust her into the car and rush right to the vet.
   b. Try to set the bone yourself and then apply a plaster of Paris cast.
   c. Splint the limb with sterile gauze and a tongue depressor or Popsicle stick, then bring her to the vet.
   d. Don't touch your cat except to confine her to her carrier or a small box and bring her to the vet.

6. Your cat has just been hit by a car. Do you . . . ?

   a. Gently pick her up, keeping her as still as possible, and head straight to the vet.
   b. Stay with her and call for help. Moving her will only make her injuries worse.
   c. Leave her where she is and run for help. You can't wait around for help to arrive. You must take matters into your own hands.
   d. Find a heavy object and mercifully finish the job the car started. It is very unlikely she will ever recover from being hit by a car, so why prolong her misery?

7. Your cat has just learned why it's bad to touch a hot stove. You should:

   a. Immediately put a pat of cold butter on her burned paw.
   b. Immediately take her to the vet. A burn is much too serious an injury for you to deal with on your own.

   c. Immediately run the affected area under cold water. If the burn looks severe, for instance, if the skin on the pad begins peeling off while you're rinsing it, take her to the vet.

   d. A cat's skin is actually quite different from yours. It's likely she won't even be affected by a burn. If she's not howling in pain, just leave her be to heal on her own.

8. Your cat has just had a bad fight with another cat in your house and you notice he's bleeding from his mouth. You should:

   a. Dab his mouth with a wet paper towel and let him go on with his day.

   b. Pry open his mouth and check for missing or fractured teeth. Take him to the vet right away if any oral damage has occurred.

   c. Pry open his mouth and pull any teeth that may have been broken in the fight.

   d. Severely punish your other cat for his unacceptable behavior.

9. Your cat has just swallowed some cleanser from under the kitchen sink. You should:

   a. Read the label on the chemical she's ingested and call Animal Poison Control at 1-800-548-2423 for further instruction.

   b. Induce vomiting immediately, before the cleanser can do any damage to her internally. Then call Animal Poison Control to see what to do next.

   c. Immediately rush your cat to the vet.

   d. Unfortunately, nothing can be done for a cat who swallows something poisonous. Her metabolism is too fast. Prepare your family for the loss of the cat and make her as comfortable as possible as you wait for the end to arrive.

10. Your cat has just stolen a chicken nugget from the kitchen table. She has unsuccessfully attempted to swallow it whole and is now choking. You should:

   a. Pat her hard on the back until she coughs it up.

   b. Try first to pull out the food obstruction with your fingers or a tweezers.

   c. Sling her over a chair and perform the Heimlich maneuver on her, just as you would if she were human.

   d. Perform an emergency tracheotomy by slicing open her throat with a clean X-acto knife and inserting a clean straw into the wound.

Answers to Quiz #33

1. B. Your cat's cuts and scrapes should be looked after, but that doesn't mean it's time to panic and hightail it all the way to the vet. You don't take your child to the pediatrician every time she scrapes her knee . . . or do you? Cuts and scrapes are a fact of life and easily heal with a little care. Clean the wound, apply a little antibacterial ointment, and if it's not bleeding profusely, leave it out in the air to heal itself.

2. D. Aside from being the best spot for getting the most accurate temperature reading on a cat, the anus is also the easiest place to take a cat's temperature. Sounds odd, yes, but think about how inclined your squirmy cat will be to hold the thermometer in her mouth, ear, or under her leg. She'll likely have it removed from any of those spots in under two seconds. The anus is a little trickier. Of course, it's not so easy to do by yourself. Enlist a family member or friend to either do the holding of the cat or the inserting of the thermometer. No one can do both! When you do take your cat's temperature, be sure to use petroleum jelly for lubrication. Insert the thermometer about an inch into the anus and wait about two minutes to remove it for a reading.

3. D. You can get the strongest pulse reading from your cat from the inside of one of her rear legs where large femoral arteries are located.

4. A, B, C, and D are all correct. (What can we say? We were feeling generous!) Some other items that will be useful in a kitty first-aid kit are basically the same you would have in a first-aid kit for human family members: sterile cotton, gauze, bandages, Q-tips, hot-water bottle, ice pack, sewing needle and thread. You may also have tongue depressors or wooden Popsicle sticks, which can be used in a pinch as makeshift splints.

5. C. The best possible solution in this situation is to try to splint your cat's broken limb with sterile gauze and a Popsicle stick, tongue depressor, or other firm object. That will keep the fractured pieces of bone from shifting and this will make your cat more comfortable. Of course, this might not be something your cat will permit you to do. In that case, your best bet is to confine her to her carrier or a small box so she can't move around too much and cause herself further pain or damage, which is what might happen if you start to panic and whisk her into the car without her being confined at all. Let your vet get a proper X-ray, see what the damage is, and set the cast. If you set your cat's limb incorrectly and it begins to heal before you get him to the vet, your vet will have to rebreak the limb to set it correctly. And you don't want that—do you?

6. B. If your cat's been hit by a car, the worst thing you can do, as above, is panic by whisking her up quickly and tossing her into your car. You have no idea how serious her injuries are, and you could make things a whole lot worse while you're trying to help. Keep calm. Gently try to move her and bring her directly to your vet. If there's any internal bleeding, time is of the essence. If your cat isn't breathing, she can be revived through kitty CPR. Place her on her side and pull out her tongue. Put your mouth over her muzzle, completely covering her nose. Gently blow and watch to see if her chest expands. If her heart isn't beating, you will also have to perform chest compressions. Breathe and do these chest compressions repeatedly for at least twenty minutes. At that point, if nothing happens, it may be too late.

7. C. Your cat does not have special skin and will feel a burn just as badly as you will. But just as it is for you, your cat won't require medical attention from your vet for a first- or second-degree burn. All that's needed is to run the affected area under cold water. A first-degree burn will show signs of redness and irritation. A second-degree burn will blister. With a third-degree burn, the skin will begin stripping off. In this case, take your cat to the vet ASAP! A pat of butter on a burn is an old wives' tale and the stuff of cartoons. Never put butter on a burn!

8. B. Missing or broken teeth could lead to infection, so for that reason, you should take your cat right to the vet if he's suffered any oral damage in a fight. Do not attempt to pull teeth from your cat's mouth on your own. Not only will you risk infection for the cat, you will also experience the wrath that made the fight so fierce to begin with. If you like your fingers, let your vet handle the dental work.

9. A. Inducing vomiting is not always the safest course of action when your cat swallows something harmful. Bringing the burning chemicals back up can actually do more harm than good. If you find that your cat has swallowed something dangerous, read the label and see what the instructions are if ingested. If vomiting is recommended, by all means, make your cat throw up. Give her a tablespoon of hydrogen peroxide, and then another fifteen minutes later. If the instructions are that she not throw up, call your vet immediately. Whatever you do, also be sure to call the Animal Poison Control center hotline at 1-800-548-2423 for further advice. Chances are, your cat can be saved, so again, don't give up until you've tried everything to save him!

10. B. Your first course of action in the case of a choking cat is to pry the object obstructing her breathing from her throat with your fingers or a tweezers. Of course, this is not always ideal. If you can't reach the food—or she won't let you reach it—then you need to administer the Heimlich maneuver, but adjusted for a cat. The idea is the same, but the procedure is a little different, owing to the different anatomy of a cat and human. When performing the Heimlich maneuver on your cat, lay her on her side. Place the heel of your hand below the last rib and push straight down two or three times.

Give yourself a point for every correct answer. SCORE:_____

Now turn to page 217 to record your score, then head to the next quiz.

34

Cat Illnesses and Ailments

A cat is there when you call her—if she doesn't have something better to do.
—Bill Adler

Chances are pretty good that within his lifetime your cat will: (a) rouse you from a deep sleep for any of a thousand reasons known only to him; (b) destroy one of your prized possessions—intentionally or not; (c) knock over your anniversary flowers; (d) get sick. These all come with the territory of sharing your life with a cat—which are, of course, easily countered by all the love and joy a cat brings to your life.

Of all of these, the fact that your cat could get sick is the most stressful by far. And it's not because some cat illnesses, like rabies, toxoplasmosis, ringworm, and others can be transmittable to humans—and vice versa. (Most cat illnesses, by the way, if contagious, are only transmittable between cats.) It's because there are things out there, sometimes beyond your control, that can cause pain, suffering, and sometimes even death for your furry friend.

It's important for every cat human to become familiar with common feline illnesses so you know what to look out for and can work with your vet to help your little guy get better. We have been able to include only some here because to list them all could be an entire book itself.

Keep in mind: Just because you can guess what may be ailing your cat does not mean you should take matters into your own hands. If your cat is exhibiting symptoms of a disease—serious or not—you still must take him to the vet to get proper medical care. Your vet is highly trained in this area; only he is qualified to diagnose and treat your cat.

So you think you know about illnesses and ailments that can plague your cat? Take the following quiz to find out.

     CAT FACT

If your cat scratches a lot at his ears, he could have ear mites. Take him to the vet right away if you notice this.

QUIZ #34

Match up the following conditions with symptoms to look for to see how much you know about feline ailments and illnesses.

a. Tapeworms
b. Kidney disease
c. Fleas
d. Rabies
e. Ringworm
f. Arthritis
g. Cataracts
h. Dehydration

i. Diabetes
j. Feline immunodeficiency virus (FIV)
k Hyperthyroidism
l. Anemia
m. Bladder infection
n. Feline leukemia
o. Heart disease

1. Typically transmitted from cat to cat through saliva and can lead to cancer of the lymph nodes, blood, abdomen, and more. Symptoms include: weight loss; fever; anemia; diarrhea; incontinence; vomiting; seizures; parasitic infections; liver, spleen, or kidney failure; and eventually death.

2. Contracted for the most part from another animal, but also contracted by humans. Symptoms include: loss of hair in circular patches, scaly skin, and deformed claws,

3 Triggered when a cat does not take in—or retain—enough water, due to illness. Symptoms include: severe thirst, increased heart rate and respiration, dry mucous membranes, decreased skin elasticity, and disorientation.

4. Transmitted from cat to cat through the exchange of body fluids. Symptoms include: secondary bacterial infections, parasites, respiratory and urinary conditions, conjunctivitis, and nervous and mental deterioration.

5. Usually transmitted by other animals. Symptoms include: excessive scratching especially at the tail and in the belly and groin areas, sores on the skin.

6. Occurring when the thyroid overproduces hormones. Symptoms include: atrophied muscles, excessive appetite, weight loss, restlessness, irritability, bulging eyes, diarrhea, vomiting, excessive urination, and high blood pressure.

7. Instigated by bacteria. Symptoms include: painful, excessive urination; irritability; restlessness; aggression; and fever.

8. Generally only present in older cats or in cats who have suffered joint injuries in their lives. Symptoms include: pain, swelling, and inflammation of the joints.

9. Caused when the pancreas fails to produce enough insulin. Symptoms include: excessive urination and thirst, excessive hunger, dehydration and diarrhea, ulcerated skin, and even coma and death if left untreated.

10. Caused by the bite of another animal. Symptoms include: restlessness; isolation; loss of appetite; fever; excessive thirst; and ultimately extreme aggression, paralysis, coma, and death if not treated.

11. Triggered primarily by impaired blood supply, infections, or metabolic disorders or age induced atrophy. Symptoms include: increased thirst and urination, weight loss and loss of interest in food, incontinence, vomiting, bad breath.

12. Sparked by hereditary conditions as well as infection, tumors, muscle disorders, nutritional deficiencies, and more. Symptoms include: breathlessness, free fluid in the thoracic or abdominal cavities, pale or bluish mucous membranes, stunted growth, underdeveloped muscles, and fatigue.

13. Caused by a reduction of red blood cells, whether by infection, bone marrow disease, parasitic infestation, internal bleeding, or malnutrition. Symptoms include: decreased appetite, weight loss, decreased activity; pale, whitish gums; diarrhea; and heavy breathing.

14. Acquired by eating raw meat or even by a flea infestation. Symptoms include: weight loss triggered by a poor appetite and diarrhea; a dry, patchy coat.

15. A typical condition of aging in a cat. Symptoms include: clouding of the eyes, decreased night vision, and decreased visual acuity.

Answers to Quiz #34

1. N. Feline leukemia, a fatal condition, cannot be cured, but it can be treated by managing all the secondary conditions that go along with it, including many types of infections.

2. E. Ringworm can be treated through topical solutions applied to infected, shaved areas of your cat's skin and specialized baths recommended by your vet. In severe cases oral medications are administered.

3. H. Mild cases of dehydration are treated in the simplest manner possible: lots of water. When it's serious, an IV with a lactated ringer's solution may need to be inserted.

4. J. Also commonly known as feline HIV, feline immunodeficiency virus is a highly contagious condition (to cats) that cannot be cured; however, treatments such as antibiotics, a specialized diet, and diet supplements may be called in to prolong the cat's life and make her as comfortable as possible.

5. C. The eradication of fleas, external parasites which feed on blood, skin, and tissue fluids, is a threefold process: (1) The fleas need to be removed from your cat with a thorough bath using a flea shampoo; (2) the fleas need to be kept off by employing a specialized flea treatment, typically a spot-on flea preventative; and (3) your home needs to be fumigated of the little buggers that hang out in carpets, curtains, and other places in the home, just waiting to get back on their furry victims.

6. K. Hyperthyroidism is treated through drug therapy and may even include surgery to remove the thyroid gland, whether in full or just a section of it. It can also be treated through appropriate doses of radioactive iodine, which will deactivate the thyroid gland.

7. M. A bladder infection, also known as cystitis, is typically treated with antibiotics.

8. F. Arthritis can be treated with anti-inflammatory drugs, and glucosamine supplements prescribed by your vet. To keep your cat as comfortable as possible, be sure to keep her weight down—to prevent excess strain on her joints—and make sure she gets plenty of exercise. Whatever you do, never give your cat aspirin or Tylenol, as these can be extremely toxic to felines.

9. I. Diabetes is not a death sentence, but if not properly looked after, it could be. In addition to a change in diet, feline diabetes is controlled with daily injections of insulin.

10. D. Sadly, there really is no 100 percent effective treatment or cure for rabies. Once infected, your cat will endure a long, painful process before succumbing. Recovery is extremely rare. For this reason, rabies is one of the best arguments for always keeping your cat indoors and appropriately vaccinated.

11. B. Kidney disease can be treated and even reversed if detected early enough. Feeding your cat a low-protein, -salt, and -phosphorus diet and ensuring he drinks plenty of water will minimize the chances that this disease will occur.

12. O. Heart disease is typically treated through medication and a change in diet.

13. L. *Anemia* may be treated by addressing the root cause if possible. It can be further helped with a change in diet as well as vitamin and mineral supplements, but in the most extreme cases, a transfusion may be necessary.

14. A. Tapeworms, internal parasites that live in an infected cat's intestines, can be treated with a worm-killing medication given by your vet.

15. G. Cataracts can be corrected but only through surgery. Cataract surgery is not recommended for all cats—especially very old cats. Talk to your vet to see if cataract surgery is safe and appropriate for your cat. He will typically refer you to a veterinary ophthamologist to perform this surgery.

Give yourself a point for every correct answer. SCORE:_____

Now turn to page 217 to record your score, then head to the next quiz.

35

Caring for a Sick or Injured Cat

People that hate cats will come back as mice in their
next life.
—Faith Resnick

As we mentioned in the previous chapter, it's inevitable that at some time in his lifetime, your cat will get sick. Sometimes the illness can be minor; other times more serious. And sometimes a cat will break a bone or damage himself in some other way. It's not enough to just know what kinds of illnesses your cat can come down with, or injuries he can get, however. It's also a good idea to know some of the ways to treat and comfort your cat once you leave the vet's office.

How much do you know about caring for a sick or injured cat? Take the following quiz to find out.

CAT FACT

A device called a pill gun can actually make getting your cat to swallow a pill easy! Ask your vet about it or look for it at your favorite pet supply store.

QUIZ #35

Answer the following statements True or False to see what you know about tending to the needs of a sick cat.

1. Your cat will always let you know if he is feeling under the weather—and just how far under the weather he feels.

2. A cat that throws up a lot could be perfectly healthy.

3. A warm, dry nose is always the sure sign of a sick cat.

4. If your cat's eyes are overly watery, it's probably just allergies.

5. An upper respiratory infection is nothing more than a common cold, kitty style.

6. To trick your cat into taking a pill, wrap it in a piece of cheese or bologna.

7. One of the best ways to dose your pill-swallowing-resistant cat with medication is to crush it up in her wet food.

8. If your vet prescribes antibiotics for your cat, your cat must finish her prescription.

9. A body temperature of 101–102°F could be very dangerous for your cat.

10. A cat that has broken or sprained a limb should be free to roam the house at will once the vet has dealt with the injury.

Answers to Quiz #35

1. False. However frisky, playful, and affectionate your cat can be, one thing she will hardly ever clue you in to is if she's in pain or feeling any kind of physical discomfort. Cats are very stoic creatures in this respect. It's instinctive for them to hide illness as a protection from predators in the wild. That's why you need to pay attention to some of the other clues she will be dropping when her health is not 100 percent, like a loss of appetite, general lethargy, soiling outside the litter box, and other symptoms we've discussed in this book.

Remember, your cat is not a complainer in the traditional sense, but if you pay attention, you'll easily pick up on her subtle signals.

2. True. While vomiting can be a sign that something is wrong with your cat, a conclusion of illness can never be drawn on vomiting alone because cats throw up for lots of different reasons. See page 140 for some of the most common triggers of vomiting for cats.

3. False. While this is a standard indicator, it's not 100 percent accurate. A cat's nose can sometimes be warm and dry if he's just tired or has been too lazy to drink anything for a while or if the environment is warm and dry. So don't rush your cat off to the vet if this is his only symptom! Rather, check back on him in an hour or so to see if his nose has returned to its cold, wet state.

4. False. Cats fall victim to many of the same allergies humans do, including pollen and dust, but for the most part, allergic reactions in cats manifest themselves on the skin. Sometimes a cat can have watery eyes due to allergies, but this is most commonly a sign of a upper respiratory infection or conjunctivitis. Pay attention to some of the other symptoms she may be exhibiting, such as how she's breathing, as well as to her eating and waste habits, and also make sure that her eyes are simply watery and not goopy. If it's just an allergy, everything else should be normal.

5. True. Symptoms of an upper respiratory infection in a cat may include: sniffles, sneezing, nasal discharge, runny eyes, fever, and hoarseness. The virus will typically run its course in seven to ten days. So yes, "upper respiratory infection" is a fancy way of saying "cold."

6. False. While this is a good way to get a big dog to take a pill, it's dangerous for cats on so many different levels that it should never, ever be considered a logical course of action. For one, both of these

foods are terrible for cats, especially the cheese, which, because it's dairy, could give your cat terrible diarrhea. Also think about the size of your cat's mouth and throat and how easy it will be for her to choke if you try and feed her a pill in this manner! What's a good way to make sure she gets the meds she needs? See below.

7. True. Crushing up a powdery pill is an effective alternative to getting your cat to take his medicine, but it has its drawbacks. For one, if your cat doesn't have much of an appetite, she may not finish her food, and therefore may not get the full dose of the medicine she needs. Also, the medication when crushed will be very bitter and ruin the flavor of your cat's food, causing her to lose interest in it. To give your cat a pill, place the pill in your hand and assume a similar posture with her as you would for trimming her claws (see page 123). Sit behind her and place her, in a sitting position, between your knees. Using the hand not holding the pill, gently hold her head back and coax her mouth open. Drop the pill to the back of her throat and close her mouth tight. With your free hand, coax her to swallow the pill by rubbing her chin and throat. This may take a few tries, so be patient. And be sure to reward her in some way once you have a successful swallow.

8. True. Even if she seems like she's feeling better in a couple of days, your cat must finish her prescription or she may actually end up getting worse. If she has a bad reaction to the pills, such as lethargy, fever, or vomiting, call your vet, who will switch her to a new prescription.

9. False. A body temperature of 101–102°F is actually quite normal for a cat. A temperature of 103°F indicates a slight fever, while anything over 105°F warrants an immediate emergency trip to the vet.

10. False. The thing about cats is that they are total troupers—but this is not always a good thing. Just as they will keep their game face on and not show pain or discomfort when they are suffering, so will they adopt an attitude of "I can do it!" when they really should not be doing much of anything. A splinted or casted cat will still think it's okay to run laps around your house, jump up on high windowsills, even wrestle with his feline friends. That doesn't mean that he should! It's your job to make sure your cat rests and heals—at least for a few days. As much as he will detest you for it, keep him confined in the bathroom or other small room with food, water, and his own litter box. Your vet will let you know when he can be free to roam and pounce and play again.

Give yourself a point for every correct answer. SCORE:_____

Now turn to page 217 to record your score, then head to the next quiz.

36

Cats in Music

As every cat owner knows, nobody owns a cat.
—*Ellen Perry Berkeley*

Philosopher, physician, and humanitarian Albert Schweitzer said, "There are two means of refuge from the miseries of life: music and cats." Anyone who knows how gratifying it is to be greeted by your feline friend when you come home at night after a trying day of work certainly knows that to be true!

Like any aspect of life, cats have made their way onto the music scene. Sometimes they have inspired compositions—other times they make their presence known in more mysterious ways.

So how much do you know about cats in the world of music? Take this short quiz to see!

 CAT FACT

T.S. Eliot's *Old Possum's Book of Practical Cats,* the basis for the musical *Cats,* was first published in 1939. Composer Andrew Lloyd Webber had grown up liking the book, but it wasn't until he came across it again in an airport book store that he got the idea to build a musical around it.

QUIZ #36

Match up the following clues about cat songs to see how much you know about cats and music.

a. The Stray Cats
b. "The Alley Cat Song"
c. "Memory"
d. Harry Chapin
e. Cat Stevens

1. He wrote and sung "Cat's in the Cradle."

2. One of their biggest hits in the 1980s was "Sexy and Seventeen."

3. The music of this famous cat comprises the soundtrack to the 1971 dark comedy, *Harold and Maude.*

4. This popular old tune has an accompanying dance that people sometimes do at weddings.

5. Barbra Streisand and Barry Manilow both covered this song from the hit musical *Cats.*

Answers to Quiz #36

1. D. Harry Chapin

2. A. The Stray Cats

3. E. Cat Stevens

4. B. "The Alley Cat Song"

5. C. "Memory"

Give yourself a point for every correct answer. SCORE:_____

Now turn to page 217 to record your score, then head to the next quiz.

37

Cats and Alternative Medicine

Thousands of years ago, cats were worshipped as gods.
Cats have never forgotten this.
—Anonymous

These days, many health professionals are seeing the value of treating their patients with alternative remedies—and that includes vets. Typically, these professionals are most accepting of a concept known as CAM, or complementary alternative medicine, which means using nature-based, Eastern healing philosophies in conjunction with more formalized, traditional, Western, science-based medical methods.

Among the hundreds of alternative remedies being used today on cats and other animals are acupuncture, massage, and herbal remedies. The field is much too broad to cover in one quiz, however, so for the sake of this book, we'll look at common herbal remedies and how they're used to treat cats.

So how much do you know about natural alternatives to traditional cat meds? Take the following quiz to find out.

CAT FACT

Recent studies have found that cats are capable of feeling fear, jealousy, grief, and love.

QUIZ #37

Answer the following statements True or False to see how much you know about herbal remedies and your cat.

1. Goldenseal is sometimes used to boost immunity.

2. Aloe vera is not dangerous for cats.

3. Calendula can be used topically to treat abscesses.

4. Echinacea is used to help prevent upper respiratory infections in cats.

5. Cat's claw is actually another name for catnip.

6. Heart conditions in cats are sometimes treated with hawthorne.

7. Foxtail is a specialized herb used to treat ear infections.

8. St. John's wort is sometimes used as a douche for cats.

9. Dandelion is sometimes used to help treat kidney disease.

10. Nettles are extremely toxic and are therefore only used to treat topical conditions.

Answers to Quiz #37

1. True. This herb is especially used for conditions related to birth and post-birth for cats.

2. False. While applied topically, aloe vera can soothe burns and skin irritations for cats, it can be very dangerous if ingested.

See Cat Toxins on page 108 for more potentially toxic substances.

3. True. Calendula stimulates healing, so a calendula ointment is best used after the abscess has been treated to help close the wound.

4. False. While echinacea is the herb of choice when it comes to fending off human colds, for cats, it is used primarily for treating existing abscesses and infections.

5. False. Cat's claw is actually a medicinal herb that comes from the rainforests of Peru and has been used for hundreds of years to treat inflammatory disorders. It has nothing to do with catnip whatsoever.

6. True. Used in its homeopathic form as the remedy Crataegus, hawthorne is useful in stimulating cardiac function.

7. False. Nope, it's not a remedy! Actually, foxtail instigates ear conditions. A spiny grass seed that can get trapped in the fur of your cat, it is sometimes known to make its way down into the ear canal, causing irritation, infection, and, in the worst-case scenario, a rupturing of the eardrum.

8. True. St. John's wort, also known as hypericum, can be mixed with water or vinegar and water to create a douche typically used to correct irregular discharge from the vulva.

9. True. Cats don't actually eat the dandelion, however; about half a dropper full of a tea made from dandelion is served to the cat roughly three times a day.

10. False. Of all the uses nettles have for humans and animals, all involve ingestion. The main uses for nettles in cats are to aid in healing of kidney disease and asthma, typically taken in the form of a tea.

Give yourself a point for every correct answer. SCORE:_____

Now turn to page 217 to record your score, then head to the next quiz.

38

Cats in Literature

A cat has absolute emotional honesty: human beings, for one reason or another, may hide their feelings, but a cat does not.
—Ernest Hemingway

Throughout the ages, cats have inspired writers and their works. Whether actual stories have been written about them—or even *by* them in some cases—the presence of cats in these tales always brings in a special dose of fun. Whether the cats are solving crimes—or writing books with their humans about solving crimes—playing, frolicking, wreaking havoc, and even mysteriously disappearing and reappearing, they are truly the stars of any work of literature in which they appear.

So how well do you know about cats in literature? Take the quiz to see!

CAT FACT
The rectal temperature is the most accurate measurement of your cat's body temperature.

QUIZ #37

Match up these famous cat characters, authors, and works to see what you know about cats in books.

a. The Cheshire Cat
b. The Cat in the Hat
c. Sneaky Pie
d. Mr. Mistoffelees
e. Midnight Louie
f. Lillian Jackson Braun

g. Garfield
h. Emily Bronte
i. Dinah
j. Cattarina
k. *Cat on a Hot Tin Roof*
l. Bustopher Jones

1. She was Alice's sleepy kitty in *Alice in Wonderland* and *Alice's Adventures through the Looking Glass.*

2. Mystery author Rita Mae Brown collaborates on her best-selling Mrs. Murphy mystery series with him.

3. She dedicated a selection of essays to one of her many cats.

4. He may possibly have been the worst babysitter of all time.

5. Edgar Allan Poe's *The Black Cat* was inspired by her.

6. He has an enormous grin and a penchant for disappearing.

7. She has written an entire mystery series that features cat detectives Koko and Yum Yum.

8. He's one of the most-published cats ever.

9. He wears white spats.

10. He solves crimes with his amateur sleuth friend, Temple Bar.

11. He's "The Original Conjuring Cat."

12. Maggie wasn't really a cat in this famous play by Tennessee Williams, but that's what they called her.

Answers to Quiz #37

1. I. Dinah

2. C. Sneaky Pie

3. H. Emily Bronte

4. B. The Cat in the Hat

5. J. Cattarina

6. A. The Cheshire Cat

7. F. Lillian Jackson Braun

8. G. Garfield

9. L. Bustopher Jones

10. E. Midnight Louie

11. D. Mr. Mistoffelees

12. K. *Cat on a Hot Tin Roof*

Give yourself a point for every correct answer. SCORE:_____

Now turn to page 217 to record your score, then head to the next quiz.

CAT YEARS VERSUS HUMAN YEARS

You know how old your cat is in chronological years, but how does that compare to your own age? Review the following chart to see!

Age of Cat	Human Years (indoor cat)	Human Years (outdoor cat)
2 months	3 years	3 years
4 months	6	6
6 months	9	9
8 months	11	11
10 months	13	13
1 year	15	15
1 ½ years	24	24
3 years	28	32
4 years	32	40
5 years	36	48
6 years	40	56
7 years	44	64
8 years	48	72
9 years	52	80
10 years	56	88
11 years	60	96
12 years	64	104
13 years	68	112
14 years	72	120
16 years	80	128*
18 years	88	136*
20 years	96	144*
21 years	100	152*

* It is rare and improbable that an outdoor cat will live more than fifteen years.

39

When It's Time to Say Good-bye

There is no such thing as "just a cat."
—Robert A. Heinlein

It's an inevitable and unfortunate aspect of befriending a cat that eventually you are going to have to say good-bye to him. There's no easy way to tell when the time has come, and then to get up the courage to actually make the appointment with the vet and go through putting him down. Anyone who's ever had to go through this knows how painful it can be.

The most important thing to remember is, however, that you are not acting as your cat's enemy and executioner. Putting an animal to sleep is a selfless act; it really does hurt you more than it hurts him. Cats especially are notorious for dealing with—and hiding—a lot of the pain and discomfort they are feeling. If your cat is expressing pain and discomfort, you can believe that it's probably very severe. If there's no way to stop the pain, it's your duty to bring him peace.

We all have the fantasy that our beloved animal will simply fall into a peaceful sleep one night, never to wake up. But this happening is actually quite rare. For a cat who passes naturally, the end typically comes with a lot of agony and discomfort; as hard as it may be to wrap your brain around by taking the proper measures to have your vet put your cat down, you are actually acting in his best interest and in the most humane manner.

DID YOU KNOW

Your cat's normal body temperature is about 101.5–102.5°F, but excitement and stress could cause it to rise as high as 103.5°F.

QUIZ #39

Please answer the following statements True or False.

1. Cats prefer to pass away naturally at home, with their family all around them.

2. A cat will know that you are putting him to sleep and he will pass away hating you.

3. Euthanasia is painful for an animal.

4. Your vet will put your cat down with an injection.

5. It will be less traumatic for your pet if you euthanize him yourself.

6. Euthanasia always occurs in the doctor's office.

7. You can be with your pet in his final moments.

8. You can take your pet's ashes from the vet's office once she has been cremated.

9. You will be able to take the body of your beloved pet from the vet's office to bury her in the backyard.

10. The best way to get over the death of your cat is to go out and get a new one right away.

Answers to Quiz #39

1. False. While this is a very romantic notion, by the time a cat has reached his final hours, he's typically not aware of very much — except that he's in incredible pain. And while his family around him will bring him some comfort, this situation is not ideal for him.

2. False. Again, by the time you get to this stage, your cat will not be aware of very much except pain and discomfort. Many humans have expressed severe guilt after they've put down their beloved cats, thinking that they could read betrayal and disgust in their cat's eyes at the very end; it's very natural to feel this way, but it's not helpful. If your cat had a wonderful life, which you know he did, he will be thinking only of all the joy and happiness he had, especially as his pain abates.

3. False. Many guilty cat owners also experience extreme guilt thinking that their cats must endure great pain in euthanasia, but, again, this is human guilt more than reality. During the process of euthanasia, your cat becomes increasingly numbed as she slips off to peace. The only pain she feels is the initial prick of the first needle. The pain you will feel is exponentially worse, but keep strong and remember this is not about you, and that you are doing the best possible thing you can for her. Giving her peace is a much greater gift than prolonging her suffering.

4. True. Sometimes the process involves just one injection; other times, there can be two or three. Initially, the vet may give your cat a sedative to relax him. This will be followed by a dose of a powerful barbiturate, which will first cause your cat to become unconscious within about three seconds of the injection. Sometimes this will be all that is needed. Other times, another dose of the barbiturate will be given to cause the brain to cease functioning and to stop the heartbeat. From start to finish, the process only takes a few minutes even though it may seem like hours.

5. False. This is an extremely bad idea for many reasons. For one, you likely do not know what you're doing, and if you try to put your cat down using various contents of your medicine cabinet, you could actually cause your cat to suffer needlessly. Moreover, is this really the kind of guilt you want to live with? It's difficult enough to take your cat to his vet and put the deed in the vet's hands; you may never be able to forgive yourself if you take it on for yourself.

6. False. While most vets will insist that the process occur in the office, for legal reasons as well as your emotional considerations, there are some who will perform the procedure in the home of the cat's family. Discuss these options with your vet, who will best be able to advise you.

7. True. You can be with your cat in her final moments, and many cat owners opt to. In addition to "being there" for their beloved friend, it also provides a sense of comfort and closure for the owner. Once your cat passes, your vet will give you a few minutes alone with your cat to say your last good-bye. But you don't have to be there. That decision is one that must be made by you. Whatever you decide, you will not be judged for your decision.

8. True. Once you've made the decision to put your cat to sleep, your vet will discuss various arrangements on how to deal with your pet's remains. Though some people want to give their pets a burial in a pet cemetery, the most common option is cremation. And yes, you will be allowed to take your pet's ashes home if that's what you decide. Your vet will explain what's involved in this process with you, but you should be able to take the ashes home with you in a few days.

9. False. While your vet can help you arrange having your pet's body transported to a pet cemetery, it is almost 100 percent likely that you will not be able to take your pet's body home with you for a backyard burial; it is actually illegal in most states to bury a pet in your backyard.

10. False. Unfortunately, many people decide the best way to cope with the pain of the loss they have just experienced is to fill the void immediately. This is not necessarily good for the human or the new animal. The next chapter looks at when the time is truly right to open your heart to a new friend.

Give yourself a point for every correct answer. SCORE:_____

Now turn to page 217 to record your score, then head to the next quiz.

40

Are You Ready for a New Friend?

Losing a pet is not *like* losing a family member, it *is* losing a family member. For many years of our lives, we become accustomed to our furry friend, the one who greets us at the door, who jumps in our lap when we're watching TV, who cuddles up next to us when we sleep. When that presence is gone, a big void is felt. And that is totally normal. You need to experience your feelings and work through your grief. Anyone who makes you feel stupid about the pain you feel at losing your cat is a heartless idiot who's probably never had a pet in their life. They're the one who isn't normal.

In your heart, no one will ever be able to replace the friend you lost. However, eventually, you may be open to the possibility of bringing a new feline friend into your life. But when is the right time to search out a new companion? That really depends on you and your family.

Before you bring someone new into your home, make sure you give yourself, as well as your spouse, children, and even other pets, a little time to grieve. There's no rush. When you give yourself time to grieve and move on, you'll be able to provide a much better home for your new cat—and you'll also enjoy a more satisfying relationship with her.

Are you truly ready for a new friend? Take the following quiz to see.

CAT FACT

A cat not only purrs when he's happy, but also when he's nervous or in pain.

QUIZ #40

Evaluate the following passages to see if you think these cat lovers are ready to bring another cat into their lives. Answer Ready, Almost ready, or Not ready.

1. Ever since I had to put down my cat, Rocco, all I can think about is holding him in those last seconds before he passed on. I'm so distressed, I even dream about it.

2. I keep thinking I see my cat, Princess, all over the house—but she passed away last week. Am I going crazy?

3. I think it will be a really good idea to visit the animal shelter on my way back from putting my cat, Patches, down this week. Maybe I'll be lucky enough to find a cat who looks just like her so it will seem like she's still with me.

4. I keep my deceased cat's ashes in a container that I can take everywhere with me. I can't seem to let go of Victor, no matter how hard I try.

5. I'm not going to tell my children that our gray cat, Smokey, is gone. I'm going to find a cat that looks just like him and pretend nothing ever happened.

6. We promised our daughter we'd look after her cat, Max, while she went on vacation, even though we just lost our Sylvester a few weeks ago and we're just not sure if we're up for it.

7. I had a long talk with my daughter last night about our Persian, Shalimar, who passed away a couple of weeks ago at age seventeen. At the end of our talk, she asked if we could get another cat, but I don't know . . . is it too soon?

8. I came home to quite a surprise last night. My wife had allowed a stray cat not only to follow her home, but to come inside the house! We lost Ginny, our beloved family cat, a couple of months ago, and at first I was a little shocked to see the new fur ball installed in the living room with the rest of the family enjoying him there. But then I got into the act and I realized how much I missed having a cat around. But are we ready for a new cat?

9. I had another dream about Lucky last night, only this time it was about her and me playing her favorite game, "kill the feather duster." I hardly ever dream about her final moments anymore.

10. I still miss Snowball, and I know I always will. But she lives on in my heart and my memories, and I can finally start thinking about her with happiness instead of sadness.

Answers to Quiz #40

1. Not ready. It's very normal to focus on these last traumatic moments for a little while. Most humans feel enormous guilt at having made the decision to put their cats down, even though their feline's condition would just get worse and worse. Getting a new cat right now is not a great idea. Instead, ask your vet if he can recommend a grief-counseling service or hotline to help yourself work through your emotions.

2. Not ready. No, you're not crazy. You're experiencing something very normal. Your heart is broken and missing your precious Princess; your head is taking the messages in and making you think she's still around to make your heart feel better. This will pass. However, if you begin interacting with your deceased cat, petting or stroking her, you may want to seek out some counseling just to make sure you're coping okay. You're also probably not ready to take in a new cat just yet. Give yourself time to heal. Soon all will be well.

3. Not ready. Heading to the shelter right on the way home from putting down your black-and-white tabby to find one with the exact same markings may seem like a good fix, but it will be temporary at best. In the long run, you may find yourself resenting the new guy for not having the same personality as your old friend, and even worse, you may not ever properly bond with your new friend as an individual. It's best to wait until the wounds have healed before embarking on a new relationship.

4. Not ready. It may upset you to hear this, but you are going to have to try harder to get over this, and it will have to start by leaving Victor's ashes alone. Transporting your cat's ashes everywhere you go isn't healthy for you, and it's actually tainting your memories of him. Remember him as he was. Your best bet is to rid yourself of his ashes, perhaps sprinkling them outside on a bush that he used to like to watch from the window. As long as you carry that box around, you will never be able to accept a new cat into your life.

5. Not ready. Just as it's not fair to fool yourself into thinking your dearly departed cat is still with you, so is it unfair to lie to your children. Kids are smart; on top of that, they likely have their own bond deeply developed with Smokey, and will know an imposter when they see one. Consider that if you're not ready to be honest with your children about your cat's passing, you may not be ready to fully cope with it yourself, and therefore, introducing a new cat into your home just now may not be ideal.

6. Not ready. The thing that's really great about having the opportunity to cat-sit a friend's or relative's cat after yours has passed is that you get to enjoy all the magic a cat can bring to your life — without committing to getting a new cat before you're ready. Enjoy playing with your daughter's cat; you may find you're ambivalent at first, but as you spend more and more time with the little fella, you may find he's just the transition you need to ready yourself for a new cat of your own.

7. Almost ready. If open communication is happening in your house and the passing of your cat is being accepted and dealt with, it may be time to start thinking about it. Just because your family members happen to be ready, however, doesn't mean that you are. Be sure to give yourself enough time to feel comfortable with the idea of a new cat before bringing one home.

8. Ready. Sometimes the best surprises are just that: You didn't know you were ready for another cat until one came and chose your family; yet everyone accepted him, which shows that yes, you're probably ready to accept another cat into your hearts.

9. Ready. You're well on your way here. You've learned to cope with the loss and are now beginning to focus on the happy times and not the sad. Now may be a really good time to consider making friends and starting brand new fun play rituals with a new cat.

10. Ready. This is just where you want to be when deciding to bring a new cat into your life. You're not looking to replace your old friend; you're not desperately trying to fill a void. You've come to terms with her being gone, and you're ready to open your heart to someone new. Provided the rest of your family is at the same place with you emotionally, the time has finally come to bring a new cat into your life.

Give yourself a point for every correct answer. SCORE:_____

Now turn to page 217 to record your score, and stay there: You're done!

Scoring

Congratulations on completing all the cat quizzes—more than 400 questions!—in this book. Now, after recording your score for each quiz you took, you're finally ready to see how you did—and how much you really do know about cats.

QUIZ #	QUIZ #
1: _____	21: _____
2: _____	22: _____
3: _____	23: _____
4: _____	24: _____
5: _____	25: _____
6: _____	26: _____
7: _____	27: _____
8: _____	28: _____
9: _____	29: _____
10: _____	30: _____
11: _____	31: _____
12: _____	32: _____
13: _____	33: _____
14: _____	34: _____
15: _____	35: _____
16: _____	36: _____
17: _____	37: _____
18: _____	38: _____
19: _____	39: _____
20: _____	40: _____

Add up your points for all of the quizzes and put your final score here:_____

SO HOW WELL *DO* YOU KNOW CATS?

0–50 points: *Cat*-atonic

When it comes to knowing about cats, you're kind of in a perpetual cat nap. Maybe you've never had a cat before, or, if you have, you clearly didn't pay that much attention to the poor critter to have learned anything from him or her. You really don't know very much about cats, but hopefully you learned something reading this book. Hey, now that you've read through it, why not take the quizzes again? Who knows — you now may know more than you think!

51–250 points: *Cat*-astrophic

So you don't know all that much about cats, but the situation isn't exactly cat-aclysmic either. There is hope for you, and if you currently have a cat, hope that he or she may still be able to live a happy life with someone who knows a thing or to about him or her. We hope that this book was able to fill in some holes in what you know about cats, and that you'll be able to use it as a reference for your future feline dealings.

251–350 points: The Cat's Pajamas!

You definitely know a thing or two about cats, and lucky for you, there's still so much more out there for you to learn. This book is only a start — a peek though a window of the wonderful world of cats. But the best way to get to know a cat is not through reading about cats, but by observing, interacting with, and loving your own cat. If you already have a cat, great! You now have 400+ new reasons to dote on her. If you don't — and heck, even if you do — there's no time like the present to head to your local animal shelter and give one of those loving little fur balls a good home. So get going!

351+ points. Cat Heaven!

You are the human companion every feline dreams of! You know when your cat needs love and you know when she needs space. Each of her meals is an absolute joy because you feed her just as much as she needs of her favorite food, and her litter box is never offensive. You are the shining example that humans can speak cat, and cats can speak human. Knowing a cat isn't difficult, you well know. All you ever have to know is *how* to listen.

About the Authors

A popular veterinarian with more than twenty years' experience, **Ronald Rosen, DVM,** is co-owner of the North Shore Animal Hospital and the South Bellmore Veterinary Group. He lives on Long Island, New York, with his wife, Mia, two children, Alex and Michelle, and *five* cats: Cody, Sabrina, Brittany, Lily, and Will.

Lifelong cat-lover **Francine Hornberger** is owner of Hornberger Publishing Services, a writing, editing, and book-packaging firm in New York City, and author of more than twenty books. She lives in Bayside, New York, with her husband, Christopher, their daughter, Madeleine, and their two cats: a giant Maine Coon named Fluffy, and Josie, a jet-black shorthaired kitten.